RENEWALS 458-4574

DATE DUE

KOREAN IMMIGRANT WOMEN IN THE DALLAS-AREA APPAREL INDUSTRY

Looking for Feminist Threads in Patriarchal Cloth

Shin Ja Um

University Press of America, Inc.
Lanham • New York • London

Copyright © 1996 by
University Press of America,® Inc.
4720 Boston Way
Lanham, Maryland 20706

3 Henrietta Street
London, WC2E 8LU England

All rights reserved
Printed in the United States of America
British Cataloging in Publication Information Available

Library of Congress Cataloging-in-Publication Data

Um, Shin Ja.
Korean immigrant women in the Dallas-area apparel industry : looking for feminist threads in patriarchal cloth / Shin Ja Um.
p.   cm.
Includes bibliographical references and index.
1. Women clothing workers--Texas--Dallas. 2. Women immigrants--Employment--Texas--Dallas. 3. Korean American women--Emigration and immigration. 4. Women--Employment--Texas--Dallas. 5. Women alien labor--Texas--Dallas.   I. Title.
HD6073.C62D358   1996   331.4'887'097642812 --dc20   96-29016 CIP

ISBN 0-7618-0463-3 (cloth: alk. ppr.)

Library
University of Texas
at San Antonio

∞™ The paper used in this publication meets the minimum requirements of American National Standard for information Sciences—Permanence of Paper for Printed Library Materials, ANSI Z39.48—1984

I dedicate this book to

    my mother CHO OK KIM and
    my deceased father the late YOUNG KUN UM

Contents

List of Figures

List of Tables

Preface

Acknowledgments

Chapter 1 Introduction	1
Theoretical Framework	3
Labor market segmentation	3
Marxian feminist theory	7
Role theory	9
Research Problem	13
Operational Definition of Variables	14
Summary	15
Chapter 2 Review of Literature	17
Patterns of Korean Immigration to the United States	17
Korean Immigrant Women in the United States	20
Married Women's Roles within the Family	22
Patriarchy and the Female Labor Market	24
Women in the Apparel Industry	28
Minority Women's Experiences in the United States	30

Chapter 3 Research Procedures	33
Methodology	35
Sampling	36
Data Collection	37
Data Analysis	38
Limitations of Study	39
Chapter 4 Research Findings	41
Korean Apparel Industry in the Dallas, Texas, Area	42
Demographic Characteristics of Sample Korean Working Women in the Apparel Industry in the Dallas, Texas, Area	44
Familial Roles	54
Work Roles	63
Social Roles	80
Perceived Health and Well-Being	92
Summary	98
Chapter 5 Korean Married Immigrant Women Working in the Dallas Apparel Industry: A Hermeneutic Approach	99
Explanation of the Motives of the Actors	100
Analysis of the Text's Structure	102
Appropriation	106
Critical Reflection	108
Chapter 6 Summary and Conclusions of the Study	111
Appendix	121
References	135
Index	145

LIST OF FIGURES

Figures
1. Peripherization of Racial and Ethnic Minorities under Monopoly Capitalist System. 6

2. The Process of the Korean Women's Role Formation 118

LIST OF TABLES

Tables
1. Asian Immigrants, by Nativity and Sex: 1990   2

2. Selected Data on the Demographic Characteristics of Respondents   45

3. Length of Residency of Respondents in the United States and in the Dallas Area   46

4. Cross Tabulation of Type of Residence of Respondents, by Year of Arriving in the United States   47

5. Respondents' Educational Attainment in Korea and in the United States   48

6. English Proficiency of the Respondents   49

7. Present Occupations of Respondents' Husbands   50

8. Comparison of Length of Working Experience in the Apparel Industry and the Present Company   51

9. Respondents' Monthly Income and Total Family Household Income in 1991   52

10. Respondents' Willingness to Give Up Working, perceived Financial Contribution, and Acceptance of Subordination to Husbands   56

11. Family Members' Housework Participation, Hours Spent Doing Housework, and Degree of Familiar Role Satisfaction of the Respondents   58

12. Sources of Child Care and Feelings about Respondents' Time Spent with Children   60

13. Respondents' Importance in the Family and Degree of Satisfaction with Family Life	62
14. Most Important Factor for the Respondents in Selecting an Employer	65
15. Respondents' Working Hours Per Week and Working Place	66
16. Respondents' Degree of the Perceived Importance in the Present Company	67
17. Respondents' Sense of Accomplishment on the Job	68
18. Perception of People's Attitude Toward Working Women	69
19. Respondents' Feelings About the Present Working Conditions and Degree of Satisfaction with the Present Company	70
20. Frequency of Job Change Among the Respondents from the Beginning to Now	71
21. Perceived Interpersonal Relationship between Employee and Employer	71
22. Possession of Medical Insurance of the Respondents	72
23. Respondents' Sense that Income is Equitable for Educational Level	73
24. Respondents' Preference of the Apparel Industry as Their Children's Future Working Area	74
25. Respondents' Perceived Social Class in the United States and Comparison of Living Conditions in the United States and in Korea	81

26. Respondents' Degree of Acceptance of Domestic Labor as a Woman's Natural Role 82

27. Cross Tabulation of Respondents' Degree of Acceptance of Domestic Labor as a Woman's Natural Role, by Respondents' Working Hours Hours Per Week 83

28. Respondents' Conception of Man's Role as Breadwinner vs. Woman's Role as Housekeeper 84

29. Cross Tabulation of Respondents' Conception of Man's Role as Breadwinner vs. Woman's Role as Housekeeper, by Respondents' Working Hours Hours Per Week 85

30. Respondents' Sense of Income Equality Compared to Men Who Have the Same Job Capacity 86

31. Respondents' Perception of Women's Status in the Family as Well as in Society 87

32. Respondents' Perception of Importance of Self in Society 88

33. Comparison of Perceived Importance of Self in the Family, in the Work Place, and in Society 89

34. Respondents' Degree of Contribution to the Korean-American Community 90

35. Success in Achieving Goals in the United States of Respondents. 91

36. Self-Rated Health Status of the Respondents 92

37. Cross Tabulation of Respondents' Working Hours Per Week by Self-Rated Health Status of the Respondents   93

38. Cross Tabulation of Respondents' Working Hours Per Week, by the Respondents' Worry About Future Illness   94

39. Respondents' Self-Rated Degree of Strength in Psychological and Physical Aspects   95

40. Direction of Respondents' Future Goal Orientation   96

41. Cross Tabulation of Direction of Respondents' Future Goal Orientation, by the Respondents' Year of Arriving in the United States.   97

Preface

As a Korean woman sociologist, I have been interested in the living conditions of Korean Immigrant women in the United States. When I proposed to do my dissertation on Korean women working in the garment industry, my advisor Dr. Valerie Bentz recognized the significance of such study, giving her wholehearted support to the idea.

Unlike most married women in Korea, most Korean married immigrant women living in the United States are working. I assumed that they would change their perception of gender roles, especially in their familial roles, because they work.

This book is one attempt to examine the effects of the work experiences of immigrant women in a new society on their perception of gender roles. This book discussed how gender, capitalism, race and ethnic minority status, and patriarchal social structure lead to the formation of new roles for Korean working women in the United States. I hope this book will help understand the hardships of many working immigrant women who are trying to adapt to a new life in the United States.

S.J.U.
February 1996

Acknowledgments

This is a revised version of my dissertation at Texas Woman's University. I would like to express my appreciation to my doctoral committee members, Dr. Valerie A. Bentz, Dr. Joyce Williams, Dr. John Marcucci, Dr. Elinor Johansen, and Dr. Rudy Seward for their advice, comments, criticism, and encouragement on the dissertation. I also would like to thank Dr. Lybe Hodges and Dr. Tae Guk Kim for their comments and critical suggestions. I would like to thank my informants in this study for their understanding and willingness to participate in this study. Without their help, this study would not have been completed. Finally, I would like to thank my family members, especially, my dear mother, who has encouraged me through many difficult times and shared my delights and frustrations.

Chapter 1

Introduction

In many cases, women's roles are often limited to the periphery of United States society as well as Asian society. Women's familial roles are generally considered as less important than the employed role of men by male-dominated society. When married women participate in the labor force, they still carry a heavy burden of family responsibilities and their work roles are usually limited to supportive positions. Some immigrant women participate in work roles which are considered as men-only roles in their home countries. While the women experience role changes, their familial roles still remain as primarily women's roles and their work roles are often ignored even by themselves. Asian immigrant working women, particularly, are faced with the additional barrier of their racial and ethnic status. These social conditions are likely to keep these women in subordinate places and create a perception of women as secondary citizens.

This study deals with Korean immigrant working women's roles in the family, society, and in the workplace. In addition, the study examines the impact of the women's roles on their perceived health and well-being. Its purpose is fourfold. First, the study describes the familial role of Korean immigrant women working in the Dallas-area apparel industry. Second, it explores the work role of the Korean women in the apparel industry. Third, it evaluates the social roles of the Korean immigrant women. Finally, it describes their perceived health and well-being. This study traces threads of feminism appearing in the process of the formation of the new role between the traditional Korean women's familial roles in Korean patriarchal society and the emerging new work roles in the United States.

The study of ethnic groups has an important history in the United States, a land of immigrants (Bahr et al. 1979). Among racial and ethnic groups, the number of Korean immigrants has increased since the Immigration and Naturalization Act of 1965 (Melendy 1977, p. 130). According to the 1990 U.S. Census, Koreans ranked fifth among Asian immigrants, with 798,849 (445,139 women) living in the United States (see Table 1). However, Koreans in the United States, especially Korean women who make up the majority (56%) of the Korean immigrants, have been the least studied of Asian immigrants. Therefore, further study of the specific problems faced by Korean women immigrants is important. Because many Korean immigrant women are employed in the apparel industry, such employees are the focus of this study.

Table 1

Asian Immigrants, by Nativity and Sex: 1990

Nationality	Population	Female	%	Male	%
Chinese	1,645,472	824,348	50%	821,124	50%
Filipino	1,406,770	756,334	54%	650,436	46%
Japanese	847,562	458,078	54%	389,484	46%
Asian Indian	815,447	377,604	46%	437,843	54%
Korean	**798,849**	**445,139**	**56%**	**353,710**	**44%**
Vietnamese	614,547	289,303	47%	325,244	53%
Cambodian	147,411	75,724	51%	71,687	49%
Hmong	90,082	44,192	49%	45,890	51%
Laotian	149,014	71,984	48%	77,030	52%
Thai	91,275	53,696	59%	37,579	41%
Other Asian	302,209	138,247	46%	163,962	54%
Total	6,908,638	3,534,649	51%	3,373,989	49%

Source: 1990 Census of Population
General Population Characteristics, United States
1990, cp-1-1

Theoretical Framework

According to Glaser et al. (1967, 3), the interrelated aims of sociological theory are "(1) to enable prediction and explanation of behavior; (2) to be useful in theoretical advance in sociology; (3) to be usable in practical applications; (4) to provide a perspective on behavior; (5) to guide and provide a style for research on particular areas of behavior." Thus, theory provides a cognitive map. It directs the handling of data and conceptualization for describing and explaining research. When it fits the situation being researched, then it can be meaningfully relevant to and explanatory of the behavior under study. The theoretical background of this research is derived from the belief of labor market segmentation, Marxian feminist theory, and role theory. These arguments are useful in understanding the present condition of labor market segmentation for minority women, the conditions of working women from a woman-centered perspective, and the impact of society on the individual self.

Labor Market Segmentation

Reich et al. (1980, 232-233) define labor market segmentation as the historical process whereby political-economic forces contribute to the division of the labor market into separate submarkets. According to the researchers, present labor market conditions can be understood by the following four segmentation processes: 1) segmentation into primary and secondary markets; 2) segmentation within the primary sector; 3) segmentation by race; and 4) segmentation by sex.

Segmentation into Primary and Secondary Markets

According to Fox et al. (1984, 79), the primary and secondary segments are differentiated by stability characteristics. The former jobs consist of professional and managerial-administrative jobs with high incomes and status, good working conditions, opportunity for advancement, and employment stability, whereas the latter jobs consist of semiskilled, operative, nonfarm labor, and service work with low incomes, poor working conditions, little chance for advancement, and lack of stability. The secondary sector is comprised largely of racial and ethnic groups as well as other minority workers such as women, students, older workers, teenagers with little job experience, the physically handicapped, and those who lack job marketability (Almquist 1979, 16). Wages for jobs with high concentrations of women are usually lower than those for comparable male jobs.

Segmentation within the Primary Sector

Within the primary sector there is segmentation between "subordinate" and "independent" primary jobs. The former occupations are routinized, disciplined, dependent upon authority, and follow goals of the organization. Both factory and office careers are present in this segment. "Independent" employments are creative, problem-solving, self-initiating, and sometimes focused on professional standards for work. In addition, voluntary turnover is high and individual motivation and achievement are rewarded (Reich et al. 1980, 233).

Segmentation by race

Reich et al. (1980, 233-234) point out that while minority workers are present in the secondary sector, subordinate primary, and independent primary sectors, they are often concentrated within distinct sectors within those submarkets. Reich argues that certain jobs are "race-typed," segregated by prejudice and by labor market institutional discrimination. The secondary sector includes factory and transport equipment operatives, clerical workers, farm laborers, private household workers, etc. (Almquist 1979, 16-17). In the early years of the migration to the United States (1870-1880), for example, Chinese workers were concentrated in mining, common labor, agriculture, manufacturing, domestic servant, and laundering (Daniels 1988, 19). The major economic concentration of another Asian immigrant group, the Japanese, is in agriculture (Daniels 1988, 163). As was true of the earlier Chinese and Japanese immigrants, a large number of recent Korean immigrants are engaged in blue-collar jobs. Even college-educated Korean immigrants are engaged as factory laborers, janitors, and gas-station attendants (Min 1988, 206).

Segmentation by sex

Reich et al. (1980, 234) also argue that job markets are segregated by gender. Incomes in the female segment are usually lower than those in the male segment. According to Fox et al. (1984, 79), 22 percent of employed women are in the upper strata of the primary sector, 44 percent are in the lower strata, and the remaining 34 percent are in the secondary sector. Furthermore, female jobs are concentrated in service-related areas, often supportive to the jobs of men. In 1989, according to Kafman (1991, 364), 64 percent of all American women workers are concentrated in the following six occupational categories: nurses and health technologists, elementary and secondary school teachers, salesclerks in retail trade, clerical workers, apparel and textile workers, and service workers such as waitresses, dental assistants, and cleaning workers. Bonacich et al. (1987, 234) state that Korean immigrant women's are concentrated in the following employment areas: nurses, operators of small businesses, garment workers, and workers in bars and night clubs. Reich (1980, 234) believes that these types of occupations are encouraged by family and educational institutions.

According to Cabezas et al. (1988, 156-162), the segmentation theory, especially based on gender and race, posits highly restricted mobility between sectors. The researchers point out that in this theory, the contents of character such as education and work experience is not considered as an important factor in the labor market. Therefore, Asian men are restricted by their race and economic class. Furthermore, Asian women, in addition to race and class, are restricted by their gender.

According to Hurh et al. (1982, 231-232), the labor-market approach to race and ethnic relations consists of two inter-linked approaches: (1) through the national economy which is focused on the class situation of black and other minorities within the structure of the United States; and (2) through the world economy which is focused on race and ethnic relations in the global context. A common point of the approach is that monopoly capitalism requires cheap labor for capital accumulation. The sources of cheap labor are either the segmentation of the domestic labor market or "surplus" or "reserve" migrant workers from the international labor market, or both (see Figure 1).

Figure 1

Peripherization of Racial and
Ethnic Minorities under Monopoly Capitalist System

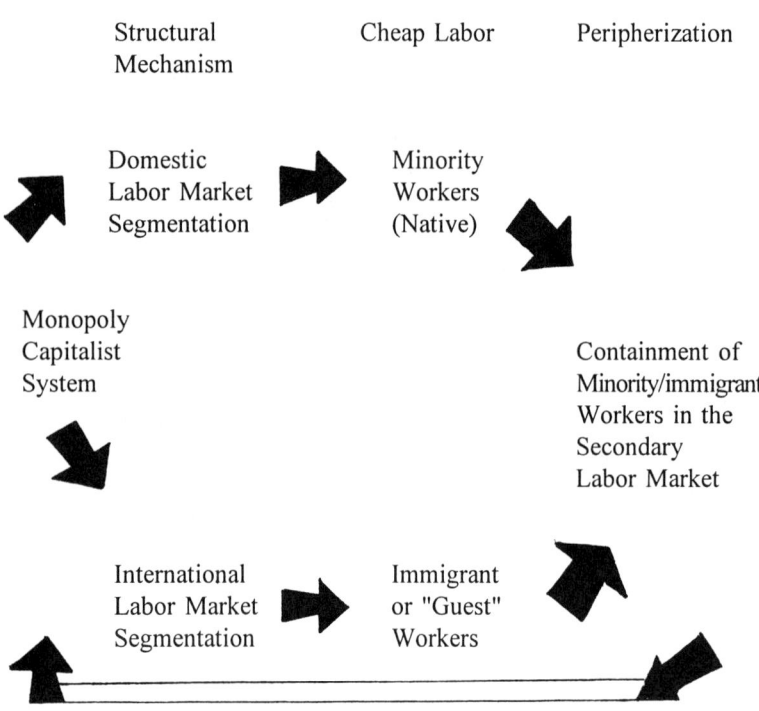

Source: Hurh, Won Moo and Kwang Chung Kim (1982), Figure 1.

Hurh et al. (1982, 234) maintain that the labor-market approach is a useful tool to examine the patterns of stratification within each minority group as well as to describe the economic conflicts among minority groups. Mitter (1986, 8-9) shows a new international division of labor in the relationship between the "Third World" which provides cheap labor and the "First World" which provides the capital. Mitter maintains that the "new international division of labor" represents a changing structure of employment from the high-wage countries of the West to low-wage, newly industrializing countries such as those in Asia and Latin America. Therefore, knowledge-intensive work remains in the United States' Silicon Valley or in Japan, while labor-intensive work is shifted to countries with cheaper labor costs.

Marxian Feminist Theory

Tong (1989, 51) maintains that Marxian feminists tend to focus on women's work-related concerns: how the institution of the family is related to capitalism, how women's domestic work is ignored, and how women are given the low-paying jobs. In *Capital*, Karl Marx (1939, 435-436) argues that modern industry throws people into unskilled and insecure conditions. Marx maintains that the division of labor in modern industry (in the early to mid-1800s) is based on the cheap labor of women, of children of all ages, and of unskilled laborers. Today's Marxian feminists focus on women's oppression as a product of the economic, social, and political structures combined with capitalism (Tong 1989, 39). These feminists view capitalism as a system of exploitative power relations.

The Marxian feminists believe that class oppression is the major factor through which gender is thrown into the pattern of patriarchy. This analysis of class provides them with the conceptual tools to understand women's oppression (Tong 1989, 42). In *Capital*, Marx states that class struggle is the outcome of exploitation of the employees by the employers, and that the labor theory of value is a principle of the derivation of the capitalist exploitation. The source of exploitation is contained in the difference between the value of labor power and the value created by labor. Marx (1939, 164-192) argues that surplus value comes from distinguishing between "labor" and "labor power." Labor is the work people actually do when they are employed by capitalists, whereas labor power is the capacity to work that the capitalist purchases from the worker. In a capitalist society, the proletarians can sell their labor power only to capitalists who own the means of production. The production of surplus value resides in the fact that proletarians are forced to work longer than is necessary to obtain subsistence, and the capitalists keep for themselves the excess value created by the laborers.

In such a society workers do not work for themselves in order to satisfy their own needs. Rather, they work for capitalists. Therefore, the workers are alienated.

Marx identifies four kinds of alienation individuals suffer in industrial labor: they are alienated from the object they produce, from their labors, from the community of their fellows, and from themselves (Coser 1977, 51-52). The workers are alienated from their productive activity. The product of their labor does not belong to the workers. The product belongs to the capitalists. The workers are also alienated from the product of their labor. The workers work only to survive. Therefore, they are alienated from their fellow workers. Finally, the workers perform less and less like human beings. Therefore, workers in a capitalist society are alienated from their own human potential (Ritzer 1988, 51-52).

In addition, Marx views industrial capitalism as having developed as the result of a variety of interrelated events. First, usury and commerce have existed throughout antiquity and have laid a basis for the primitive accumulation of capital. Second, the exploration and exploitation of the New World brought great wealth to a few people. Finally, Marx points to the emergence of a system of public credit and its expansion into a world-wide credit system (Turner et al. 1989, 161).

Cox's concept of a "World-System" helps us understand how Marx's capitalism works in present-day capitalism. Hunter et al. (1987, 223) maintain that the origin, growth, and development of a world-system perspective on capitalism was developed by Cox. Cox attempts to link the internal organization of national units and the international system. Cox believes that the two levels of analysis constitute the world capitalist system. Cox (1964, 198) argues that the workers in the advanced capitalist nations will advocate reform rather than revolution, and the employers in the preindustrial countries will be antagonistic to the demands of the workers.

Marxian feminists tend to focus on the division of labor in the family and gender inequality in society. In the *Everyday World As Problematic*, Smith (1987) shows how women have been alienated and exploited by male-centered society. Smith (1987, 18-20) points out that women have worked as much as men, but women have been excluded from the work of producing the forms of thought and the images and symbols. Women's experience has not been represented while men's views are represented as universal. She describes the situation in our society:

> Only one sex and class are directly and actively involved in producing, debating, and developing its ideas, in creating its arts, in forming its medical and psychological conceptions, in framing its laws, its political principles, its educational values and objectives. Thus a one-sided standpoint comes to be seen as natural, obvious, and general, and a one-sided set of interests preoccupy intellectual and creative work (Smith 1987, 20).

Dalla Costa (1972) maintains that women should demand wages for housework. In her study of "Women and the Subversion of Community," she urges that a major source of alienation in women is isolation in the home and dependency on men. She finds that factory labor is less alienating than housework because of its collectiveness. Hartmann (1981, 25), in "The Unhappy Marriage of Marxism and Feminism," argues that "the family allows the control of women's labor by men both within and without the family." Hartmann (1981, 8) also maintains that demanding and getting wages can raise women's consciousness of the importance of their work.

Tong (1989, 45-46) points out that Marxian feminists believe that the Marxist theory of politics offers an analysis of class in which women are oppressed economically and socially. Under capitalism people are free to do what they want to do, but they have little to say in determining the limitations of the system. According to Tong, however, under communism, people are not only free to do what they want to do but are also free to shape the structure of their system. Marxism holds to the idea that both women and men should fulfill their full human potential. Tong (1987, 47) believes that the goal of the Marxian feminist is to identify the operation of gender relations as the processes of production and reproduction as understood by historical materialism.

Role Theory

The main focus of role theory is the impact of society on the individual self. On a micro level, it is concerned with how society is constructed from individual roles (Collins 1988, 234). Mead's notion is that the self is a social product (Mead 1934, 140). According to Mead (1934, 135), "The self . . . arises in the process of social experience and activity, that is, develops in the given individual as a result of his relations to that process as a whole and to other individuals within that process." The self comes out of a society and interaction with other selves. Mead uses the baseball game as an example to explain and elaborate the combination of different roles in society. In baseball, one does not act out a highly specific individual role. The player must continually adjust his or her behavior to the needs of the team as a whole and to the specific situations that arise in the game. A role set refers to the combination of different roles that any particular individual plays. Most people play one or more roles in different spheres such as home, work, community, and so forth (Collins 1988, 236).

Scanzoni (1970, 19-21) approaches family cohesion from the interaction at two levels: the instrumental level which includes economic provision and household work, and the expressive level which includes companionship, empathy, and affection. In one-earner families, husbands provide income, that is, the instrumental-level role, while wives take care of the household and children on the expressive level. Scanzoni reports that a satisfactory exchange of instrumental-level roles motivates an exchange on the expressive level. He maintains that two-earner families can be more cohesive than one-earner families because the wife's economic contribution provides additional factors for instrumental exchanges between husbands and wives (1970, 104-105). But Voydanoff (1987, 15) wonders whether wives' labor-force participation outside of the home is followed by an increase in husbands' participation in domestic work inside the home. Voydanoff (1987, 16) argues that men have not shared the same degree of involvement in women's traditional roles in family work as women have shared in their new provider role.

Several research studies show the impact of work and family roles on American women's physical and mental health (Voydanoff 1987, 80-81). Performing multiple roles is generally correlated with good physical health (Kother et al. 1989; Lois Verbrugge 1983; Nathanson 1980), while specific combinations of work and family roles are negatively correlated to health (Haynes and Feinleib 1980). According to Kotler et al. (1989), women with a multiplicity of roles, such as employed, married women with a child present in the home, have the lowest risk of mortality while women with few roles, such as unemployed, unmarried women with no child at home, have the higher risk of mortality.

In "Multiple Roles and Physical Health of Women and Men,"

Verbrugge (1983, 16-30) surveyed multiple roles and the physical health of white adults (18 and older) residing in the Detroit metropolitan area in the fall of 1978. According to the Detroit data, employed, married fathers with work, marriage, and parenthood roles tend to have the best health, while employed non-married mothers involved in the roles of work and parenthood tend to have the best health. The worst health is shown among non-employed married fathers, men with none of the three roles, and non-employed married men without children. In the case of women, women with none of these roles have the worst health. Verbrugge's study (1983) shows that the combination of fulfilling job and family roles has no negative impact on health. Another study supporting a positive relationship between multiple roles and good health is Nathanson's (1980) analyses of data from the U.S. Health Interview Survey. His research concludes that married women and women with children report their health more positively and report lower levels of illness behavior and fewer chronic conditions than women in other family role categories.

Work by Haynes et al. (1980) did find multiple roles to affect negatively the physical health of women. In "Women, Work and Coronary Heart Disease: Prospective Findings from the Framingham Heart Study," Haynes et al. (1980) found that although employment is not related to the incidence of coronary heart disease in women, working women who have ever been married, have raised children, and have been employed in clerical work are at increased risk of developing coronary heart disease. According to Voydanoff's (1987, 81-82) research, the effects of performing multiple roles on the mental health of women are similar to those for physical health. Those women who are married, are employed outside the home, or are mothers have low levels of depression (Aneshensel et al., 1982; Kandel et al., 1985; Ross et al., 1988). Those who are married and employed also report fewer psychophysiological complaints than unmarried and unemployed women, even though women with minor children at home have more complaints (Gore and Mangione 1983).

A study by Aneshensel et al. (1981) in Los Angeles County during 1979 shows the relationship of family and work role to gender differences in terms of depression. According to the Los Angeles study, women tend to suffer more depression than men for all employment categories (full-time, part-time, unemployed, or retired). Full-time employment is reported to benefit both males and females, and unemployment is reported to have enormous negative effects for both men and women. In general, gender differential in depression increases as family role obligations increase. However, the parent groups tend to have lower depression scores than unmarried-employed and single parents, although this is more apparent for men than for women.

The Kandel et al. (1985) study supports the conclusion that being a parent is associated with fewer depressive symptoms than not being a parent. Occupational and household roles are associated with the highest levels of stress. In an urban community in the Northeast, the researchers tested the effects of strains and stresses on well-being in marital, household, and work roles. The research shows that the family roles with strain deriving from interpersonal conflicts are the most stressful variable considered. Most of the strains identified in marriage are related to interpersonal conflicts. In general, a lower level of depression shows among those who are married, parents, and workers. Especially among women, those who have the most complex role configuration, such as married, employed, and parent, report the lowest levels of depressive symptoms.

According to a study by Gore et al. (1983), the absence of employment or marriage is found to be related to depression for both men and women. In "Social Roles, Sex Roles and Psychological Distress: Additive and Interactive Models of Sex Differences," the researchers examine the relationships between gender, social roles, and symptoms of psychological distress through an analysis of survey data from a metropolitan sample. In this research, they report that non-working married women with children have higher levels of distress than working married men and all working women. In general, the presence of both employment and marriage have a positive influence on psychological health for both men and women. Ross et al. (1988) report that levels of psychological well-being for employed mothers are higher than those of mothers who are not employed. According to the researchers, depression of employed wives is affected not by children, but by the difficulty of arranging child care and by the husband's lack of participation in child care. Employed mothers who are supported by family members for child care have lower depression levels than those who use other types of arrangements.

Research Problem

The research problem for this work is to describe 1) the demographic characteristics; 2) the familial, work, and social roles; and 3) the perceived health and well-being of Korean immigrant women working in the Dallas area apparel industry. More specifically, the following research questions are addressed under each of five specific categories.

1. What are the demographic characteristics of Korean immigrant women working in the Dallas apparel industry?

    a. What are the familial characteristics (see definition below) of Korean immigrant women working in the apparel industry?

    b. What are the work characteristics (see definition below) of Korean immigrant women?

    c. What are the social characteristics (see definition below) of Korean immigrant women?

2. What are the familial roles among the Korean immigrant women who have had apparel company employment?

    a. What is the perceived impact of Korean immigrant women's employment on their families?

    b. How do Korean immigrant women satisfy their familial roles?

3. What are the work roles among Korean immigrant women in the apparel industry?

    a. How do Korean immigrant women get into the industry?

    b. What are the working conditions of the Korean immigrant women in the apparel companies?

4. What are the social roles among Korean immigrant women?

    a. How do Korean immigrant women describe their lives in the United States?

    b. How do Korean immigrant women perceive their positions in society?

5. What is the perceived health and well-being among Korean immigrant women?

    a. How do Korean immigrant women perceive their state of health?

    b. How do Korean immigrant women perceive their well-being?

Operational Definition of Variables

Familial characteristics refers to the marital status, number of children, spouse's present occupation, and number of workers within the family (see questions 1-4 in the questionnaire included in the appendix).

Work characteristics refers to the length of working experience in the apparel industry, length of working experience in the present company, and kinds of work skills (see questions 5-7).

Social characteristics refers to the respondent's age, education, proficiency in the English language, length of residence in the U.S., length of residence in the Dallas area, former occupations in Korea, current income, and household composition (see questions 8-20).

Impact of employment refers to the woman's perceived financial contribution to the family (see question 21).

Familial role satisfaction refers to all family members' housework participation, hours spent in housework, level of necessity for financial contributions, child care, feelings about time spent with children, number of hours shared with children, number of hours shared with family, degree of satisfaction with family life, familial role satisfaction, degree of equality with husband, and the importance of self in the family (see questions 22-33).

Korean immigrant women's entrance into the industry refers to job information and selection of a company (see questions 34-35).

Working conditions refers to working hours, working place, job benefits, kind of work presently performed, working conditions, job satisfaction, gender equality, frequency of job change, income satisfaction, attitude toward working women, the importance of present position, interpersonal relationship between employee and employer, advantages and/or disadvantages of the job, and any problems in the apparel company (see questions 36-59).

Korean immigrant women's lives in the U.S. refers to comparison of living conditions in the United States and in Korea, and income satisfaction (see questions 60-61).

Korean immigrant women's perceived positions refers to the perceived importance of self in society, degree of contribution to the Korean-American community, conceptions of women's role, perception of women's present status, perception of social status, and goals to achieve in the United States (see questions 62-71).

Perceived state of health refers to any illnesses, number of days sick, number of days absent from work, a self-rating of health, and worry about future illness (see questions 72-76).

Perceived state of well-being refers to the women's self-rated degree of psychological and physical strength, and direction of future goal orientation (see questions 77-79).

Summary

The purpose of this study is to describe the familial, work, and social roles and the perceived health and well-being of Korean immigrant women working in the Dallas apparel industry. The theoretical background of this study is derived from the theory of labor market segmentation, Marxian feminist theory, and role theory. Reich et al. (1980) define labor market segmentation as the historical process whereby political-economic forces contribute to the division of the labor market into separate submarkets. Marxian feminists focus on women's oppression as a product of the economic, social, and political structures combined with capitalism (Tong 1989). The main focus of role theory is the impact of society on the individual self. Several research studies indicate the impact of work and family roles on women's health. Performing multiple roles is correlated with good physical health in studies by Kother et al., Lois Verbrugge, and Nathanson, while specific combinations of work and family roles are negatively correlated to health in work by Haynes and Feinleib. The research problems addressed concern the demographic characteristics, the familial, work, and social roles and the perceived health and well-being among the Korean immigrant women. In the following chapter, pertinent literature on Koreans and Korean women will be reviewed.

Chapter 2

Review of the Literature

The following six areas will be discussed in this review of the literature: (1) patterns of Korean immigration to the United States; (2) Korean immigrant women in the United States; (3) married women's roles within the family; (4) patriarchy and the female labor market; (5) women in the apparel industry; and (6) minority women's experiences in the United States.

Patterns of Korean Immigration to the United States

The first group of Korean immigrants to the United States began coming in December 1902 when 121 Koreans left for Hawaii aboard the S.S. Gaelic, and arrived at Honolulu on January 13, 1903; during the next three years, a total of 7,226 Koreans in 65 groups left Chemulpo, now Inchon, for Hawaii (Yun 1977, 33). Hurh et al. describe three factors that encouraged the emigration of Koreans to Hawaii at the beginning of the 20th century (1984, 39-40). The first factor was the economy. In 1901 a nationwide famine took place in Korea, caused by an unusual drought followed by floods. The Korean government imported large amounts of grain from foreign countries, but many people faced starvation. By then the Korean government was willing to relax its traditionally tight restriction on emigration. The second factor was the fact that Hawaiian plantation owners needed the Korean laborers and encouraged emigration. The third factor was the influence of the American Christian missionaries and of Dr. Horace N. Allen, then the American minister in Seoul, Korea. The Reverend George H. Jones told his fellow Christians and the Korean people that America was a Christian country and that Hawaii was the paradise of the Pacific, where the weather was good and working conditions were excellent.

The first Korean immigrants to Hawaii included various social classes. Unlike Chinese and Japanese immigrants, who were mostly peasants, only one-seventh of the Korean immigrants were peasants while the others were common laborers, coolies, low-grade government officials, ex-soldiers, students, house servants, mine workers, and political refugees. Korean peasants in that period were too conventional to join the emigrant group. Also peasants emigrated in small numbers because emigration was advertised only in big cities and port cities.

The first Korean immigrant group included 56 male laborers, 21 women, 13 children, and 12 babies (Kim 1977, 110). Kim quotes (1977, 110-111) Kim Won-young in reporting that a total of 7,226 Koreans came to Hawaii before the Korean government put an end to its liberal emigration policy in November of 1905. Among these people, there were 6,048 men, 637 women, and 541 children. Another source, however, reports that a total of 7,843 Koreans immigrated during the same period: 6,701 men, 677 women, and 465 children.

According to Kim's (1986, 13-19) research, during the second period of immigration, between 1906 and 1945, only a limited number of Koreans came to the United States as "picture brides," students, etc. The reasons for the lack of population growth among Korean immigrants were combined with the pressure of the Japanese government to halt Korean immigration and the institutionalized racial discrimination of immigration policy in the United States. First, the Japanese government was under pressure from Japanese immigrants in Hawaii to stop Korean immigrants who took their places as strike-breakers (Kim 1986, 16). Japanese were at first welcomed but their demands for high wages turned California growers against Japanese immigrants (Daniels 1988, 109). Second, the Japanese government discouraged Japanese immigration to alleviate the anti-Japanese movement in the United States. In addition, Japan, which occupied Korea beginning in 1910, pressured the Korean government to ban emigration in exchange for Washington's continued support for Japanese immigration (Kim 1986, 16). Third, an American immigration quota was levied against non-Europeans, especially Asians, during the period 1924-1965. Under the Immigration Act of 1924, the formation of families in European-immigrant communities was supported (Takaki 1989, 14). European-immigrant men were allowed to return to their home countries and bring wives to the United States under non-quota status. Until around the end of World War II, however, no quota was allowed for Asian countries because of the discrimination clause included in the Act: "No alien ineligible for citizenship shall be admitted to the United States." (Hurh et al. 1984, 40-41)

During the second period, there was a strong drive for Koreans to become involved in organizations. For example, between 1905 and 1910, more than 20 organizations were created among Koreans in the United States. Among them, the United Korean Society in Hawaii and the Mutual Assistance Society in the mainland United States were two major organizations. They merged into the Korean National Association on February 1, 1909. The objectives of the association were to promote educational and business development in the Korean community, to protect Koreans' rights, and to support the movement of Korean independence. During this period, churches also became a major factor as a place where Korean immigrants exchanged information, shared their culture, strengthened their identity and satisfied their spiritual needs.

The third period of Korean emigration, from 1946 to 1964, was influenced by internal as well as external factors. The immigration of Koreans resumed with the defeat of Japan in 1945, but information on the number of Korean immigrants to the United States between 1945 and 1947 is not available in any source (Kim 1977, 11). According to the United States immigration report, 46 and 40 Korea-born immigrants came to the United States in 1948 and in 1949 respectively. The United States government's military support during the Korean War (1950-1953) developed strong ties between South Korea and the United States (Kim 1986, 18). The war brought some Koreans into the United Sates under special categories. Between 1950 and 1964, an average of 2,834 Koreans came to the United States. annually. During the period, immigrants represented 35.4 percent of all Korean people entering the United States (Light et al. 1988, 131). Three major groups of Koreans came to the United States. The first consisted of Korean students, those who were selected by the Korean government to study at the universities in the United States. More than 10,000 of these students came to the United States after the end of the Korean War, but only a few of them returned to Korea. The majority of the Korean students (7,542) adjusted their visa types in the United States from student to permanent resident. The second group of Koreans were immigrants consisting of large numbers of "war brides" who followed their husbands back to the United States after their having served with the military in Korea. The third group consisted of thousands of Korean orphans or deserted children, who were born during the war to Korean women and soldiers of the United States. These children were brought to the States to be adopted.

The current movement of Korean immigration to the United States began with the passage of the 1965 Immigration Act. Since that law made provisions for the spouses, children, and parents of citizens in the United States to come as non-quota immigrants, the number of Koreans coming to the United States was tremendously increased. According to the 1970 U.S. Census, there were only 70,598 Koreans in the United States; by 1980, there were 357,393 Koreans, but in 1990, the number of Koreans reached 798,849. Kim (1986, 19-20) points out how the immigration law affects the number of Korean immigrants coming the United States, and how it affects the process of adaptation and assimilation of the Korean immigrants in the United States.

Although the Korean community in the United States has grown rapidly because of immigration in recent years, its residential distribution and mobility have received scant attention from social scientists (Hurh et al. 1984, 61). The main difficulty for researchers is that major Korean immigration to the United States is so recent that no official statistics are available, especially in the Dallas area. According to the 1990 U.S. Census, 31,775 Koreans reside in Texas and 7,290 in Dallas. But these numbers are assuredly low because the size of the Korean community in Dallas increases every year.

Korean Immigrant Women in the United State

According to a study by Yang (1987, 167-168), approximately 2,000 Korean women came to the United States between 1903 and 1924. The Korean woman's role was very important, especially in the early stage of adaptation in the United States. In their native land of Korea, women held subordinate positions to their husbands; in the United States, Korean women could become equal in status to their spouses.

Yang (1987, 168-173) classifies the early Korean women's economic participation in the United States into two periods: 1903-1910 and 1910-1924.

Except for the few "warrior" women who came to the United States with their children in defiance of their husbands' wishes, the Korean women who came to the United States in the first wave were a group of people who simply followed their husbands. Between 1903 and 1910, their motherland of Korea was suffering poverty, heavy taxation, and exploitation by Japanese merchants. Therefore, some Koreans considered emigration to be a good opportunity for economic security as well as for their children's future education (Yang 1987, 168-169).

According to Yang's research in 1987, almost 40 percent of the early Korean female immigrants were Christian converts. However, these immigrants were also traditional Korean women who were deeply rooted in the Confucian philosophy. In the early settlement years, the life of Korean immigrants was characterized by hard work and frequent moves seeking better conditions. The first jobs of the Korean immigrants were as sugar plantation field workers in Hawaii. The daily wage was 65 cents for the men and 50 cents for the women. The average time of women's labor was 10 hours a day, 6 days a week. In addition, women had domestic responsibilities such as cooking, cleaning, and sewing. Some women earned a living by running boarding houses for Korean bachelors. Even though the work of the boarding house was demanding, the income was better than that earned by working in the field. Korean immigrant women contributed financially to the stability of families. This was vitally important for survival in the unfamiliar environment of the United States.

Between 1910 and 1924, 951 "picture brides" arrived in Hawaii and 115 came to the mainland of the United States from Korea (Yang 1987, 171). "Picture brides" refers to the practice of "sending the bachelors' pictures to prospective brides in their home towns, and letting the girls choose their mates" (Choy 1979, 88). The story of picture brides reflects the courage of young Korean women in the face of very closed-minded Korean rural community attitudes in the early 20th century. About 80 percent of the approximately seven thousand Korean immigrants who entered Hawaii were bachelors (Choy 1979, 88). Since Korea is a family-oriented society, the Korean-Hawaiian workers' living conditions in Hawaii were seen as unstable. Thus the marriage problem was not only an individual problem but also a social issue within the Korean community in Hawaii in terms of population increase and community stability. Finally, someone suggested the idea of picture brides to solve the problem. Before picture brides came to the United States in 1910, the sex ratio within the 20 to 39 age category in Hawaii was extremely unbalanced (1,380 males to every 100 females). Because of the arrival of picture brides and the maturation of Korean women who came to the United States in the first wave of immigrants, the sex ratio within this age category was reduced to 225 males for every 100 females in Hawaii and about 300 males to 100 females on the mainland of the United States (Yang 1987, 172). The early Korean immigrant women contributed to their families in psychological and economic terms.

The United States was not close to Korea geographically, culturally, or psychologically in the early 1900s. The early immigrants who established a successful Korean-American immigrants' history were pioneers (Um 1990). In the United States, the women overcame oppression in the multiple areas of culture, class, race, and gender (Chai 1988, 53).

Married Women's Roles within the Family

Pleck (1982, 101) argues that when women perform two roles (one in addition to the family) they encounter considerable problems of strain and exhaustion, while men's family life is not affected at all. According to Pleck (1982, 106), two dominant patterns exist in male and female roles in marriage. The first is a traditional pattern in which husbands cannot tolerate their wives' taking any paid employment. The second is a recent pattern in which husbands can accept their wives' employment when it does not come close to or surpass their own in prestige.

In 1890 in the United States, only 4.5 percent of married women were working (Smith 1979, 3). By 1970 it was 41 percent (Statistical Abstract of the U.S. 1989); by 1978 it was nearly half (Smith 1979, 3); by 1980 it was about 51 percent; by 1984 it was 54 percent (U.S. Congress 1984, 1); and by 1988 it was 57 percent (Abstract of the U.S. 1989). Although the number of married women in the labor force increased, married women still remained primarily responsible for child care and other domestic work (McAllister 1990, 83) while the husbands' family roles remained unstable (Pleck 1982, 108).

A number of studies have been published on the effects of women's work force participation on their household work. In "Gender and Household Labor: Employment and Earnings Variations in Australia," McAllister (1990, 88) reports that males do some 10 hours of household labor per week, while females do 32 hours per week. Married women with children do about 40 hours of household labor per week, women who are widowed do 28 hours, divorced or separated women do 25 hours, married women without children do 23 hours, and women who have never married do 15 hours. By contrast, married men with children do some 12 hours of household labor per week, men who are widowed do 21 hours, divorced or separated men do 13 hours, and men who have never married do 9 hours. These data indicate that males are less affected by domestic labor burdens than are females.

Fox et al. (1984, 182) point out that even though many employed people are able to manage the house, they feel less certain about the care of children. Yet social research has supported the idea that maternal employment does not negatively affect children and marriages (Nieva 1985, 164). One study indicates that children do not suffer from the mother's employment (Fox et al. 1984, 182). Rather, working women's experiences have increased the woman's sense of well-being and potential and the woman's power in the marriage (Nieva et al. 1981, 45). In addition, the financial resources contributed by the wife's job enhance the family's living conditions and social class position (Nieva 1985, 164). However, working wives do not receive significantly more help in household work from their husbands than do non-working wives. Vanek (1980, 87-89) points out that husbands of employed women give no more help than husbands of non-employed women.

In "The Dual Career Family: A Variant Pattern and Social Change," Rapoport and Rapoport (1969, 8-23) report five foci of stress in married working women. The stress factors are overload dilemmas, personal norm dilemmas, dilemmas of identity, social network dilemmas, and role cycling dilemmas. Nieva et al. (1981, 48) state that women can lessen role conflict by the elimination of some roles and the combination of work and family roles. The researchers found that the more responsibilities a woman has at home, the more work-family conflict she will experience. McAllister (1990, 80) maintains that since more women are entering the labor force and remaining there after marriage, the interrelationship of the domestic and the economic spheres is likely to assume greater significance in labor markets.

In 1979, Kim and Hurh (1987, 204-212) studied Korean immigrant women's labor-force participation and the division of household tasks in the Los Angeles area. A total of 615 adults (218 males and 335 females) participated in this study. The researchers found a high proportion (68%) of labor-force participation and a traditional pattern of household task performance among Korean married women. The division of household tasks was examined in terms of the role behavior and role expectations of family members. The household tasks included grocery shopping, housekeeping, laundry, dishwashing, disposal of garbage, and management of the family budget. Types of division of household tasks were classified into the following three categories: 1) wife performs predominantly, 2) husband performs substantially, and 3) children or other family members are involved.

In the Kim and Hurh study, one-third of the married respondents (155, 32%) reported that the husband alone is employed, while more than half of the respondents (261, 54%) indicated that both husband and wife are employed. The researchers found that the majority of married women, those with and without children, perform the following four tasks: grocery shopping, housekeeping, laundry, and dishwashing. The study also shows that the husbands of employed wives do not perform the tasks more than do husbands of the non-employed wives. Kim and Hurh (1987, 213) conclude that Korean immigrant working wives carry a heavier burden from their working roles and familial roles than wives in Korea or non-Korean wives in the United States.

In another research study which is entitled "Korean Immigrant Working Women in the Early 1980s," Bonacich et al. (1987, 232-234) report that more Korean immigrant wives and mothers have participated in the labor force in the United States than in their native country of Korea. The researchers point out that Korean immigrant women work as much as, if not more than, native women of the United States. Yet they still participate in a patriarchal family culture which assumes that women are not in the labor force. Therefore, Korean immigrant working women appear to be suffering from a double workload, accompanied by friction in the household.

Patriarchy and the Female Labor Market

In "The Origin of the Family Private Property and the State," Engels

(1972, 136-137) argues that the legal inequality of the two partners in marriage is the result of the economic oppression of women. Engels maintains that the modern family is based on the open domestic slavery of the wife. According to Engels, the husband has a responsibility to support his family, and that in itself gives him a superior position to his wife. "Within the family he is the bourgeois, and the wife represents the proletariat."

Patriarchy is defined by Lim (1983, 76) as male domination of the economy, society, and culture. Women's inferior status results from patriarchal institutions and social relations. Discrimination against women comes out of the patriarchal assumption that a woman's natural role is a domestic one; therefore, she is not suited to being a salaried employee. Lim (1983, 77-78) points out that the limitations on women's employment opportunities are related to the attitudes of families, employers, and women themselves; limitations also grow out of domestic responsibility and women's own lack of skills.

Feminists argue the same point of universal gender difference and inequality. Mitchell (1974, 412) views patriarchy as the fundamental ideological structure of the family. She maintains that patriarchy operates mainly in the psychological realm where female and male children learn to be women and men. Hartmann (1981, 12) points out that Mitchell failed to give patriarchy a material base in terms of women's and men's relationships in the labor force. Hartmann (1981, 18-19) defines patriarchy as "a set of social relations which has a material base and in which there are hierarchical relations for men and solidarity among them which enables them in turn to dominate women." Hartmann sees the following factors as elements of patriarchy: heterosexual marriage, female child rearing and housework, women's economic dependence on men, the state, and institutions based on social relations among men. Hartmann (1981, 15) maintains that the foundation of patriarchy lies in men's control over women's labor. The material base of patriarchy rests in the family as well as in the social structure. Hartmann (1981, 5-16) points out that increased oppression of women is related to exclusion of women from wage work. Men control women's labor by excluding women from access to some essential productive resources. Mitter (1986, 144) maintains that in the ideology of a patriarchal family, a woman's primary role is considered to be in the area of household labor. Therefore, women's work outside the home is seen as a secondary role by society and by the family. Even though women put in many hours in their work, the female worker is always seen as a "permanent casual."

In *The Second Sex* de Beauvoir (1957, xv) states that a man never begins by presenting himself as a person of a certain sex, but when the author defined herself, she had to mention that "I am a woman." In the relationship of the two sexes, man represents both the positive and the neutral while woman represents the negative. Woman is not considered as an autonomous being. According to de Beauvoir (1957, xvi), "She is defined and differentiated with reference to man and not he with reference to her; she is the incidental, the inessential as opposed to the essential. He is the Subject, he is the Absolute--she is the Other."

Eisenstein (1983, 5) maintains that the term "patriarchy" is an inappropriate word to characterize the situation of women in the modern society. She defines the term as the "universal" oppression of women by men. Eisenstein (1983, 7-8) believes that the sense of one's gender is produced psychologically and socially, rather than physiologically. She emphasizes the importance of the environment in determining the distinction between sex and gender. Sex means the biological sex, whereas gender means the culturally and socially shaped expectations, attributes, and behaviors assigned by the society. Gender distinction depends on the varied expectations of behavior and character formation for men and women from culture to culture. Levi-Strauss (1969, 496-497) also theorizes that women's subordination is crucial to the formation of any culture. His study has contributed to a shift of attention from the economic system to the symbolic and meaning systems of societies.

Millett (1970, 228-230) researches gender attributes of female and male. She reports that for the female, "normal" meant passive, while for the male, it meant active. The traits of men are found to be tenacity, aggressiveness, curiosity, ambition, playfulness, responsibility, originality, and competitiveness; while the traits of women are affection, obedience, passiveness, responsiveness to sympathy and approval, cheerfulness, kindness, and friendliness. Social pressure keeps women exhibiting the expressive traits while men perform the instrumental traits. Eisenstein (1983, 11) points out that sex roles are a form of oppression, keeping women restricted and limited in their scope.

Weedon (1987, 2) refers to patriarchy as power relations in which women's interests are subordinated to the interests of men. She points out that behind the sexual division of labor and its implication for the equality of women and men lies a fundamental patriarchal assumption of the biological difference between women and men. Weedon (1987, 3) maintains that patriarchal relations are structural and exist in the institutions and social practices of our society, for example, the family, schools and colleges, teenage fashion and pop culture, the church, and the worlds of work and leisure. Phelps (1981, 17) views patriarchy as a structure of authority relations between women and men. Phelps maintains that patriarchy is the whole system of male authority which makes women's positions secondary to men's.

Fox et al. (1984, 34-37) argue that occupations become segregated into male jobs and female jobs. About 25 percent of all female workers are in the general categories of secretaries, household workers, bookkeepers, elementary school teachers, and waitresses. Almost 40 percent of all female jobs are related to the general categories of typist, cashier, nurse, and seamstress. In addition, the researchers report that the domination of certain occupations by men are shown in the overall labor force. Moreover, traditional female jobs provide few promotion opportunities and little or no on-the-job training. Rothman (1987, 191-192) points out that full-time female workers' average weekly income in 1983 ranged somewhere between 65 percent and 68 percent of male workers' income. More specifically, for example, in sales work, women earned 51 percent of the amount earned by men; in executive jobs, 64.2 percent; in clerical jobs, 68.8 percent; and in the professions, 71.9 percent.

Discrimination against women in the labor force is a widespread phenomenon, even today. Blau et al. (1985, 31) maintain that in each year, women are represented largely in clerical and service jobs, while men are more likely to be managers and supervisors. Discrimination in the labor market exists even in the case of equally qualified men and women (Blau et al. 1985, 40). Hartmann (1981, 26) describes the wage difference between the sexes as part of a patriarchal system in which the male has control of women's labor. Hartmann believes that the wage differential supports women's secondary position to men as well as women's economic dependency on men. Therefore, according to Hartmann, the gender division of labor in the labor market should be understood as a manifestation of patriarchy.

Women in the Apparel Industry

Enloe's (1983) research shows how the textile and garment industries have depended on female labor through time. According to Enloe's (1983, 409) historical research, in 1896, more than 87 percent of French clothing workers and 51 percent of all textile workers were women; in the Soviet Union in 1970, 85 percent of textile workers and 93 percent of "sewing industry workers" were women; in Hong Kong in the early 1970s, 80 percent of the garment work force were women; in Canada in 1971, 90.1 percent of all sewing machine operators were women; in Tunisia in 1972, 74 percent of textile workers were women and in Britain in 1976, 45.2 percent of all textile workers were women and 72.5 percent of all workers in leather, footwear and clothing manufacturing were women. According to Enloe's (1983, 410) research on labor costs in the garment industry in the late 1980s, Belgium paid an average of $8 an hour, the United States $4, Britain $3, South Korea 45 cents, Egypt 36 cents, and Pakistan 28 cents.

According to Coyle's (1982, 18) research, absenteeism, high turnover, and poor working conditions have become characteristic of the clothing industry. Hoel (1982, 84) reports that the labor force in clothing manufacturing in Coventry is exclusively immigrant women workers who are economically and socially vulnerable and have difficulties in obtaining better jobs in the labor market. His research shows that a great number of women have moved two or three times in a two-year period to improve their wages and conditions as well as to escape from the constant harassment and abuse of employers.

Vazquez (1981, 86-87) states that, the apparel industry is the sixth largest manufacturing industry in the United States, and 71 percent of the industry is concentrated in eight states. The eight leading states are New York, Pennsylvania, California, North Carolina, New Jersey, Georgia, Texas, and Tennessee. The apparel companies tend to be small, about 65 percent having fewer than 50 workers. Minority workers make up 17 percent of the industry's labor force. Compared to U.S. manufacturing as a whole, apparel manufacturing remains a highly labor-intensive industry. According to a 1991 U.S. Department of Commerce report, female employees make up 77 percent of the workers in the apparel industry, compared with 33 percent for all manufacturing. Minority workers have approximately double the representation in the apparel industry that they have in manufacturing as a whole. The industry is very sensitive to such labor-related issues as immigration law changes, minimum wage legislation, and unionism (U.S. Dept. of Commerce 1991, 34-2). Coyle (1982, 10-11) points out that as a labor-intensive industry the clothing industry is dependent on cheap labor. Low capital investment contributes to the industry's hand-to-mouth existence, with narrow profit margins because of competition within the industry.

Sung (1976, 151-152) points to the garment industry as one source of jobs where Chinese immigrants can easily enter as seamstresses. The nature of the job is unpleasant, characterized by low-income piece work, long working hours, and poor working conditions. In "The Domestic Clothing Workers in the Mexican Metropolis and Their Relation to Dependent Capitalism," Alonso (1983, 169-170) argues that the domestic seamstresses of Neza are superexploited by Mexican monopoly capital. The workers' salaries are lower than the minimum legal wage, and their working hours are more than eight hours a day. The clothing industry does not offer any kind of social benefits to its employees. In addition, because of its seasonal character, the clothing industry offers very unstable jobs. Alonso (1985, 162) insists that the lack of scientific research regarding such domestic industries in other Latin American countries might be due to the clandestine nature of the phenomenon, imposed by the structural organization of the garment industry itself. Mitter (1986, 50) cites the working conditions of the garment and textile industry as highly hazardous to health. According to Mitter, byssinosis or brown lung is common among workers.

In "Korean Immigrant Working Women in the Early 1980s," Bonacich et al. (1987, 238-240) point out that the garment industry depends largely on female labor. According to the researchers, garment factories are absolutely dependent on the wage labor of employees. The workers, predominately women, are hired to sew pre-cut garments on a contractual basis. The researchers argue that "the garment industry was a notorious exploiter of labor" (1987, 239). Home-workers are often paid by the piece, rather than by the hour because, according to the researchers, an inexperienced sewer would take more time than an experienced operator to make a garment. If the sewer is paid by the piece, hourly wages fall below the minimum wage. In addition, when sewers work in their homes, it is not possible to know the number of hours they work to earn their wages. Coyle (1982, 19) also points out that piece work is a way of pushing wages down, rather than a system of reward for increased productivity.

Bonacich et al. believe that the economic conservatism of the garment industry's manufacturing is greatly expanded by the subcontracting structure of the industry. Also, the use of female labor in the garment industry decreases the likelihood of unionization, because women's responsibilities for home and children reduce the time they have to devote to organizations. As a result, segments of big business in the United States are beneficiaries of the exploitation of immigrant women. The researchers conclude that cheap female immigrant labor helps the United States garment industry remain competitive. An additional beneficiary is the broad class of consumers who are able to purchase clothing cheaper. If the prices of basic necessities could be kept in check, then wages could also go down.

Minority Women's Experiences in the United States

Minority women face double burdens from their racial and ethnic status and their gender. Zavella's (1987) research on cannery workers in the Santa Clara valley shows how Chicanos have been discriminated against in terms of their gender and race. Zavella (1987, 35, 57-59) points out that even though 47 percent of in the cannery labor force is women, only 3 percent of the female workers have the highest-paying jobs. Through apprenticeships or company policies, male workers have a chance to be promoted; however, female workers have no job ladder. In addition, there are two labor forces in canneries: the year-round, skilled, or supervisory positions which are occupied by white men and the lower-level or seasonal positions which are occupied by Mexican-American women.

According to statistics (Fox et al. 1984, 153-156), the largest proportion of minority women workers in the United States are blacks, followed by women of Spanish origin, and finally by women of Asian origin. Filipino women have the highest labor-force participation rates among all women. Among married women, Japanese women have the highest labor-force participation rate. Filipino women are highly represented in the health professions. Japanese and Chinese women also have a sizable number in the primary labor force, such as high school teachers (Almquist 1979, 138). Chinese, Japanese, and Filipino women are often employed while Indian, Mexican-American, and Puerto Rican women are not (Almquist 1979; Fox et al. 1984). However, women of Asian origin are heavily concentrated in the lower-level professional and technical jobs. In general, according to Almquist (1979, 138), minority women are very poorly represented in managerial jobs; instead they are highly represented in the secretarial and service jobs. Almost a third of Asian women are employed in the secondary labor markets. Fox et al. (1984, 156) point out that the dual oppression of racism and sexism is a major factor in minority women's status in the labor market. The researchers argue that a significant reason for the job market success of some Asian-American women can be found in their acculturation in the United States; that is, the longer Asian-American women reside in the United States, the more they accept American gender roles and reject the traditional patriarchal structure.

Hughey (1990, 383-389) maintains that median incomes for female immigrants are influenced by the following eight variables: educational attainment, English language proficiency, female labor-force participation rate, male labor-force participation rate, average number of children per woman age 35-44, average family size, marital status, and the proportion of all immigrants living in a Standard Metropolitan Statistical Area. Using data from a special tabulation of the 1980 Census, Hughey (1990) studied the incomes of females from 59 countries who entered the United States between 1970 and 1980. Hughey found that English language ability and educational attainment are among the important determinants of women's incomes. High female labor-force participation rates are reflected in higher family incomes. Male labor-force participation rates, on the other hand, have an inverse relationship to female income. An additional child and/or elderly relatives in the home can cause a reduction in a woman's earnings. Married women tend to have higher incomes than unmarried women, with lower labor-force participation. The variable of residential area is affected by income. Place of residence for the vast majority of immigrants seems to provide a good chance for employment. Finally, motivation and cultural characteristics of the immigrants are variables related to income, even though relationships were not found to be significant.

Throughout the review of the literature, the following six areas were discussed: patterns of Korean immigration to the United States; Korean immigrant women in the United States; married women's roles within the family; patriarchy and the female labor market; women in the apparel industry; and minority women's experiences in the United

States. In summary, the number of Korean immigrants in the United States has increased rapidly in recent years and women make up almost 60 percent of these immigrants. The women's financial as well as psychological contributions play important roles in Korean survival in the United States. However, when the women perform familial roles as well as work roles, they may suffer from their double workload (Kim and Hurh 1987; Bonacich et al. 1987).

The concept of gender is a product of the social and psychological realm rather than the physical realm. Women's inferior status results from patriarchal institutions and social relations (Lim 1983). Hartmann (1981) maintains that the gender division of labor in the labor market should be understood as a manifestation of patriarchy. A high concentration of female employees among workers in the apparel industry is understood as a result of this structure. According to Boancich et al. (1987), garment factories are absolutely dependent on the wage labor of employees. Cheap female immigrant labor helps the United States garment industry remain competitive. Thus, minority women face double burdens from their racial ethnic status and from their gender.

Literature relevant to minority women workers in the apparel industry in the United States is scarce. There is no study available on Korean immigrant women working in the apparel industry in the Dallas area. Therefore, the study of Korean immigrant women's roles in the family, society, and the workplace will contribute to an understanding of their conditions in relation to gender and their immigrant status in the United States. This research will also help to determine how the structure of patriarchy works in regard to the women. The next chapter will include a description of the research procedures used to examine and to describe the women's roles and the effect of their roles on their perceived health and well-being.

Chapter 3

Research Procedures

This chapter addresses research procedures and limitations of the study. The research procedures describe the methodology, sampling, data collection, and data analysis. For the purpose of this study, the research problems were focused on the multiple roles and the perceived health and well-being of Korean immigrant women in the Dallas apparel industry.

A multi-method approach to the research problem is used. The multi-method approach, often called triangulation, provides different bits of information that can supplement one another. There are some advantages to the use of the multiple method. Often, if findings cannot be combined, it is not known how to interpret some of the information. The different aspects of information need cross-checking to verify the validity of observation (Gorden 1987, 12). The methodology used in this study is Denzin's "triangulation." The research method includes use of a questionnaire, in-depth interviews, and field notes.

Labaw (1985, 12-13) defines a questionnaire as a totality, a gestalt that is greater than the sum of its individual questions. According to him, each part of a questionnaire includes elements vital to every other part; therefore, all the components must be integrated and handled simultaneously. There are two types of questions: open-ended and closed-ended. Open-ended questions allow the respondent to represent the depth of his or her feelings on controversial issues. Depth of feeling does not show up accurately in closed-ended questions (Labaw 1985, 135). Closed-ended questions, on the other hand, allow easy statistical analysis. However, in many cases the researcher cannot understand what the answers actually meant to the respondent. In these questions, the inferences are hidden; the researcher can ignore them, while, in an open-ended question, the answer by the respondent gives the researcher the ability to peer into the respondent's head (Labaw 1985, 143-144). The questionnaire for the present research will consist of both open-ended and closed-ended questions.

Wiseman et al. (1970, 32) maintain that the information obtained through in-depth interviews and observation will stimulate the researcher to conduct a broader survey on a larger sample of respondents using a questionnaire. Observation is useful for gaining insight into a respondent's habitual activities (Wiseman et al. 1970, 17). A researcher uses the in-depth interview, rather than observation, when he or she decides that the interview is the only way to know the subject's mind. Through the in-depth interview, a researcher goes into details about social interactions and interrelated attitudes. In addition, a researcher can obtain information that cannot be anticipated (Wiseman et al. 1970, 30).

The methods of data analysis in this study include descriptive and hermeneutic approaches. According to Wiseman et al. (1970, 38), the descriptive statistics focus on the range and distribution of such social characteristics as age, sex, occupation, and marital status. This analysis can determine how characteristics are related to a particular behavior pattern or attitude. For this research, the range and distribution of roles will be described, and roles correlated with perceived health and well-being. Throughout the process, the characteristics of each role and the effect of the roles on the perceived health and well-being are presented.

The hermeneutic approach is based on the historical meaning of experience and its developmental and cumulative effects at both the individual and social levels (Polkinghorne 1983, 203). A hermeneutic approach clarifies meanings which are concealed by abstraction and thus the consequences that follow from them (Linge ed. 1976, 11). The in-depth interview with Korean working women in the Dallas apparel industry, field notes from the workplace and home setting, and the questionnaire research findings of the women will be used as texts for hermeneutic investigation.

Methodology

Denzin (1978, 291) maintains that "the sociologist should examine a problem from as many different methodological perspectives as possible." To avoid biases from a single methodology, "triangulation," a multi-method approach, is used in this study. This is the combination of methodologies to examine a problem from as many different perspectives as possible.

According to Schutz (1976, 16-17), to be a social scientist, the observer ought to have his or her mind free of any practical interest in the social world and should restrict his or her motives to the honest description and explanation of the social world observed. To do this, according to Schutz, the researcher can distribute questionnaires, hear witnesses, and establish test cases. But the researcher's theoretical task may be directed by the researcher's information about the social world. Schutz (1976, 81-82) shows how to construct "ideal types of actors," also called "puppets," who are created and manipulated by the social scientist. The scientist observes certain events within the social world and begins to formulate a typology of such events. Later the scientist adjusts these typical acts and constructs a personal ideal type which he or she imagines as having consciousness. But the personal ideal type does not have the task of mastering the world. Then the question might arise, "Why not simply collect empirical facts?" Schutz (1976, 85) answers that to understand social phenomena, we have to understand them within the categories of human action such as human motives, planning, means, and ends. Therefore, the social scientist should ask what happens in the mind of an individual actor.

The methodology of the present research includes library research (presented in the literature reviews), survey research, and field research. For the survey research, a questionnaire and in-depth interviews were administered. For the field research, complete observations were collected and analyzed. In addition, the present research includes Ricoeur's hermeneutical approach, defined as the theory of the operations of understanding in their relation to the interpretation of texts (Ricoeur 1981, 43). Ricoeur (1978a, 101) states that the purpose of interpretation is to overcome a remoteness and a gap between the past to which the text belongs and the interpreter himself or herself. The interpretation can be clearly defined by overcoming the distance. "Every hermeneutics is thus, explicitly or implicitly, self-understanding by means of understanding others" (Ricoeur 1978a, 101). Hermeneutical theory tries to solve the problem of how meaning can be understood objectively or how to avoid misunderstanding (Bleicher 1980, 215).

Sampling

A non-random sample of 74 Korean immigrant women who are working in Dallas area Korean apparel companies was selected. Because of the lack of information regarding the Korean apparel companies, it was not possible to get a comprehensive listing of Korean apparel companies in the Dallas area. Therefore, this study was conducted using a non-random sample rather than a random sample. The respondents of this study were selected from Korean apparel companies listed in the Korean Texas Garment Contractor's Association and Korean newspapers. The researcher called or visited the apparel companies for the data collection. The researcher also contacted ex-employees and sewing employees whom the researcher knows well. A snowball technique was used to select the respondents who were willing to participate in this study. Respondents were asked to provide names of other Korean apparel companies known to them.

A sample size of 100 women workers was originally projected. One-hundred-fifty questionnaires were distributed. Of these, 13 percent were administered in the Korean apparel industry in Irving, 27 percent were in Carrolton and in the industrial area of Harry Hines Boulevard in Dallas, 35 percent were in the Garland area, 20 percent were in Korean churches, and 15 percent were distributed to respondents' homes. About 46 percent of the respondents refused to cooperate. Seven questionnaires had to be discarded because of incomplete data. The final sample for this study consists of 74 respondents.

In addition, the researcher contacted four employers, two managers, two ex-employees, and five sewing employees (including two home sewers) in garment companies or in homes for in-depth interviews. Two employers, two managers, and two employees were solicited as respondents when the researcher visited apparel companies for data collection. Two ex-employees and three employees were introduced to the researcher by persons who knew their experiences in the apparel industry. All of the respondents who participated in the in-depth interview showed interest in this study which facilitated the interview.

Data Collection

The present research includes use of a questionnaire, in-depth interviews, and field notes from a complete observation. In the complete observation, a researcher "observes a social process without becoming a part of it in any way" (Babbie 1989, 266). The questionnaire was administered to a sample of 74 Korean immigrant women who worked for a Korean-owned apparel company. The questionnaire consists of 32 open-ended and 47 fixed-choice questions. The questionnaire was translated into Korean. The research instrument was administered by the researcher and an assistant, both of whom are native speakers of Korean. The respondents were contacted individually in their homes, workplaces, or churches. Each respondent had a copy of the questionnaire in Korean, and the researcher explained directions for its completion. Since it is known that 90 percent or more of the total population in Korea is literate (Bureau of Public Affairs 1987), it was assumed that most of the Korean immigrant working women would be able to read the questionnaire and write the answers. The respondents were given a period from one to 3 weeks for its completion. During that period of time, the researcher visited or called the respondents at their sewing companies or at their homes to encourage them to complete the questionnaire. The Korean responses were translated into English by the researcher. The data collection process took approximately 6 months, from March to August of 1991.

Glaser et al. (1967, 162-163) maintain that the main point of field work and interviews is to see the concrete situation and informants in person. These researchers (1967, 3-6) suggest that systematic discovery of theory from the data of social research is the best approach to generate theory. Examples of theory based on data are Weber's theory of bureaucracy and Durkheim's theory of suicide.

The present research also used in-depth interviewing which "enables the investigator to probe the intensity of an individual's feelings about a given social phenomenon..." (Wiseman et al. 1970, 27). In the in-depth interview, respondents often indicate their judgments regarding others' attitudes and the influence of the others on their own attitudes and behavior. Wiseman et al. (1970, 28) maintain that memories of past events can be collected through the in-depth interview. In-depth interviews were conducted with 13 informants. For the in-depth interview, two immigrant women who had experience working in an apparel company during their early stages of living in the United States were contacted individually in their homes. Two home sewers were also contacted individually for interviews using the questionnaire and informal interviews. Four employers, two managers, and three sewing employees in apparel companies were contacted individually in their workplaces. These interviews took half an hour to 2 hours. Each was recorded in notes or on audiotape. The notes or audiotapes were later translated into English by the researcher. Selections from the notes and audiotapes that have significant meaning to the research subject were made for hermeneutical analysis.

In addition, complete observations from the workplace and home setting were conducted. For the observations, two Korean apparel companies were selected in Garland and Irving, and two home sewing places were selected non-randomly. When the researcher visited apparel companies for data collection or interviewing, the researcher also conducted a complete observation regarding the present working conditions of the companies. The complete observation data were collected as systematic field notes. Furthermore, a selection of field notes was made for hermeneutical analysis. Field notes were selected for their relevance to this study and their validation of its other findings.

Data Analysis

The data from the questionnaires were analyzed using quantitative procedures available through SPSSx computer programs. Descriptive statistics, including frequency tables and cross tabulation charts, were used. Probability statistics were not used because of the non-random nature of the sample. Qualitative procedures were used to analyze categories which emerged from the data themselves. Field notes from the complete observation were analyzed in terms of hermeneutical theory. The field notes, and recorded notes and audiotapes from in-depth interviews were used as a text for hermeneutical interpretation. The following four steps of Ricoeur's hermeneutics were applied: (1) explanation of the motives of the actors; (2) analysis of the text's structure; (3) appropriation; and (4) critical reflection. Ricoeur believes that the theory of text-interpretation offers a better understanding of people and the being of all beings (Ricoeur 1967, 355). According to Klemm (1983, 140), the moment of appropriation is the final stage of the hermeneutical process, because at this stage the meaning of the text is clearly defined.

Limitations of Study

There are two primary limitations to this study. First of all, there are few previous studies of Korean-immigrant women's working conditions in the apparel industry in the United States. Therefore, information concerning Korean women in the apparel industry is limited to the Dallas area. Second, a problem of reliability can be raised from the nature of this study, which is based on a non-random sample with 74 respondents. A comprehensive listing of Korean apparel companies in the Dallas area is not available; therefore, it was not possible to conduct a random sample.

Keeping these limitations in mind, the following chapter will discuss research findings. More specifically, it will address analytic integration of findings, descriptive analysis, case presentations, and the researcher's observations.

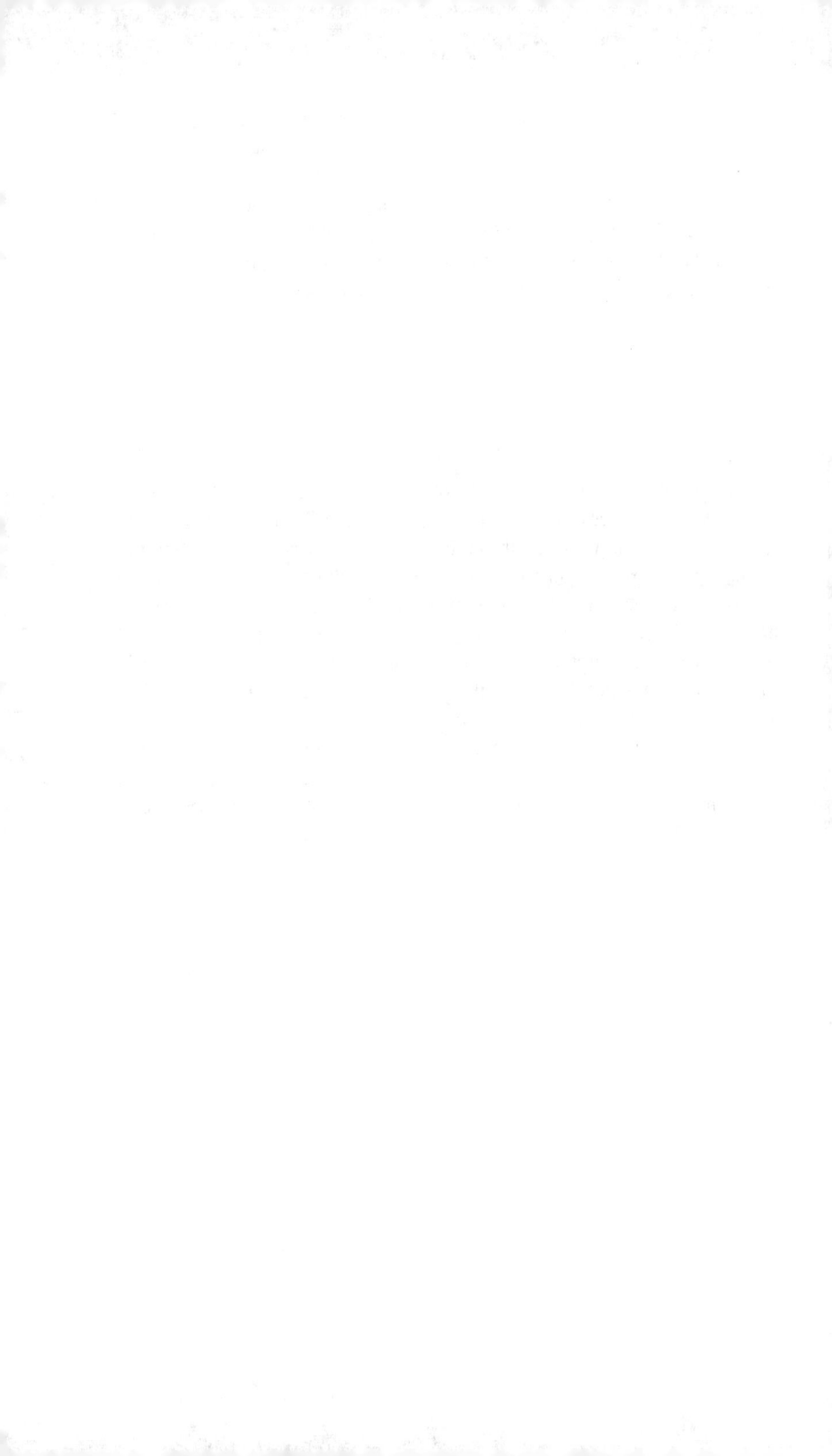

Chapter 4

Research Findings

The objective of this study is to investigate the familial, work, and social roles and the perceived health and well-being of Korean immigrant women working in the Dallas-area apparel industry. Five research questions were posed concerning immigrant Korean women and (1) their demographic characteristics, (2) their familial roles, (3) their work roles, (4) their social roles, and (5) their perceived health and well-being. This chapter describes the Dallas area research findings in these five areas.

During the period from 1974 to 1990, the Korean women who are the focus of this research arrived in the United States from Korea. Their major goals were to achieve financial success for their families and scholastic success for their children. The women began working to achieve these goals with sewing jobs. In their native country of Korea, opportunities for the employment of married women are not open in all areas, even for those who are high-school educated. Thus, the economic activities of married women are very limited in most cases. Compared to employment conditions in Korea, conditions of employment for married women in the United States seemed not only different but better. The women were highly motivated to become employees in the United States; however, they were not very marketable. More than 95 percent of them had no education at all in the United States, and their ability to use the English language was minimal. The Korean women did not have much knowledge about the United States and most also had minor children. Under these conditions, the women's employment resources were largely limited to other Korean Immigrants.

Korean Apparel Industry in the Dallas, Texas, Area

According to Young K. Lee, president of Korean Texas Garment Contractor's Association, there are 23 apparel companies in the association. Each industry employs approximately 10 to 15 permanent employees, more than 90 percent of whom are women. Not surprisingly, most of the managerial positions in the Korean apparel industries are filled by Korean males. The Korean apparel industries are located in Garland, Irving, Carrollton, and in the Harry Hines Boulevard area of Dallas, where they can obtain a potential labor force of Korean immigrants. Since working hours are flexible and it is possible to work at home, many Korean women immigrants have worked or still do work in the apparel industry. The Korean immigrants are interested in working in the apparel industry because they believe their families will benefit by the income they earn. Most of the time, Mr. Lee believes, the family life suffers because the women cannot devote as much time to caring for the family as they did in the past. Mr. Lee, whose wife works in his company, said that his family has suffered from his "workaholic" wife. He seemed to be very dissatisfied with his wife's long working hours.

Through interviews with employers, managers, ex-employees, and sewing employees in garment companies, I was able to sketch briefly an account of the garment companies' businesses, as well as different aspects of problems. A manager described a sewing business as follows: The working hours are from 7:00 a.m. to 10:00 p.m., Monday through Friday. There is no sick-leave policy. The manager's main jobs are to check in and check out garments, to make schedules to get ordered garments out within a certain period, and to inspect garments before delivery to a main company. Usually the company makes a month's contract for 500 pre-cut pieces of garments from a main company. For this period, the company arranges 3 weeks for sewing and a week for finishing the ordered garments. Pre-cut pieces of garments are distributed to employees who are working in the company and/or at home.

Recruitment for the company is through advertisements in Korean newspapers. Because of the nature of the work, which requires ordered garments to be completed by a certain date, there is no fixed number of employees. Positions in the company are always open. Sewing positions of employees are arranged by their work experience and skills. Sometimes sewing skills are tested in the initial interview. Within the apparel company, jobs are classified into two types: sewing and other jobs such as handsewing, trimming, ironing, hemming, picking threads, making button holes, attaching buttons, folding, packing, etc. The other jobs are often called "shiage." Most Asian women, including Korean women, prefer to have sewing, rather than other, positions. Wages vary from $3 to $8 per piece. More experienced, skilled women, those who have 5 or more working years in the apparel industry, usually make samples or complete clothes and are paid more. Less experienced women make a simple piece or a part of a garment. Sometimes they are paid less than $2 per piece. The pay reflects labor-market segmentation of immigrants with low wages in a labor-intensive enterprise. The other jobs, which are called "*shiage*," are held mostly by Mexicans and a few elderly workers. These jobs are paid by the hour beginning with minimum wage. Working hours are flexible. The working place is also flexible, either at the factory or at home.

Most women enter the apparel industry through their Korean friends, relatives, or neighbors. The apparel industry is very easy to access because it does not require any qualifications to apply. In the apparel industry, the women began to learn how to sew. The learning process requires great patience in order to overcome obstacles such as physical pressure from long working hours and psychological conflict arising from the difference between their dreams and the reality of their experiences in the United States. But the women's strong desires to achieve their major goals enables them to endure many hardships. Through the relationships with other Korean workers in the apparel industry, the Korean women learn how to adjust in a new world that is totally different in language, culture, and custom. In addition, their financial contributions provide a base on which to build their families' financial stability. No doubt, however, the patriarchal structure of the garment industry causes unequal opportunity and inferior positions for Korean women in the workplace. The following demographic data indicate that the women are a relatively homogeneous social group.

Demographic Characteristics of Sample Korean Working Women in the Apparel Industry in the Dallas, Texas, Area

The age distribution of Korean women in this study ranges from 20 to 53 years. The median age is 38, and the mean age is 38.3. More than half of the Korean women who were given questionnaires are in their 30s; about one-third of them are in their 40s. As shown in Table 2, the majority of the Korean women are married; about 8 percent are divorced; about 5 percent are single; and about 3 percent are widowed. All of the women over 30 are or have been married, while none of the women below 25 is married. The divorce rate of 8.1 percent of the women is almost the same as the divorce rate of 8.2 percent of the women in the United States in 1988 (U.S. Department of Commerce 1990, 43). More than half of the women indicate a nuclear type of family, living with their husbands and/or their children. About 11 percent report a matrifocal type of living with their children, and about 10 percent indicate an extended type of living with their spouses, children, and mothers. Only one woman lives alone.

According to Table 2, almost 70 percent of the Korean married women have two or more children; the modal number of children is two. The average number of children is 1.9. About 12 percent of the women have no children. The age distribution of the children is presented in Table 2. About 44 percent of the women have minor children under 12 years old, while about 23 percent of them have adult children over 18 years old. The Korean women's children range in age from 1 to 34. The median age is 16 years and mean age is 12.6 years. As shown in Table 2, almost 60 percent of the women live in rented homes, while about 40 percent of them own their homes.

Table 2

Selected Data on the Demographic Characteristics of Respondents

Characteristics	N=74	%
Age		
20-29	6	8.2
30-39	38	51.3
40-49	24	32.4
50+	6	8.1
Marital Status		
Currently married	62	83.8
Divorced	6	8.1
Never been married	4	5.4
Widowed	2	2.7
Number of Children of*		
the Married Respondents'		
0	8	12.1
1	13	19.7
2	31	47.0
3	14	21.2
Children's Age Distribution*		
Under 6	19	18.8
7-11	25	24.7
12-17	34	33.7
18 and over	39	22.8
Home Ownership*		
Own	29	40.8
Rent	42	59.2

*These characteristics exclude missing observations.

Table 3

Length of Residency of Respondents in the United States and in the Dallas Area

Year of Arrival	In the U. S. N	%	In the Dallas Area N	%
1974 - 1979	17	23.3	16	21.9
1980 - 1985	22	30.1	16	21.9
1986 - 1990	34	46.6	41	56.2
Total	73	100.0	73	100.0

Missing observation=1

All of the Korean women came to the United States between 1974 and 1990. Almost half of the women came to the United States between 1986 and 1990; and more than half of them came to the Dallas area during the same period. The majority of them has about 5 years experience living in the Dallas area, as indicated in Table 3. The Korean women's average length of residence is 7.2 years in the United States. The length of time in Dallas is 6.5 years. According to the 1980 Census, 81.8 percent of all Koreans in the United States were foreign born, and their average length of residence in the United States was a little more than 5 years. In the 1990 Census, the percentage of foreign-born Koreans decreased to 72.7 percent but still the majority of Koreans in the United States were foreign born.

Table 4

Cross Tabulation of Type of Residence of Respondents, by Year of Arriving in the United States

Type of Residence	Year of Arrival in the U.S.			Total (%)
	1974-79	1980-85	1986-90	
	N	N	N	
Own house	13	12	3	28 (40.0)
Rented house	3	9	30	42 (60.0)
Total (%)	16 (22.9)	21 (30.0)	33 (47.1)	70 (100.0)

Missing observations=4

The length of time the Korean women have been in the United States seems to be associated with the type of residence, as indicated in the cross tabulations of Table 4. The women who have lived in the United States for 5 years are more likely to own a house, while those in the United States fewer than 5 years are more likely to reside in a rented house.

Table 5

Respondents' Educational Attainment in Korea
and in the United States

Education	in Korea*		in the U. S.	
	N	%	N	%
None	0	0.0	71	95.9
Completed elementary	2	2.8	0	0.0
Completed middle school	13	18.1	0	0.0
Completed high school	50	69.4	0	0.0
Some college	2	2.8	1	14
College student	0	0.0	2	2.7
Completed college	5	6.9	0	0.0
Total	72	100.0	74	100.0

*Missing observations=2

All of the Korean women received at least some education in Korea; the modal educational attainment is "completed high school." More than 95 percent of the women had no education at all in the United States. In this study, only three women (including two current college students) reported some college education in the United States. This study shows workers in the garment industry are composed mostly of the first generation of immigrants who were not educated in the United States.

According to the 1990 census, 74.1 percent Korean women had a high school or higher and 25.9 percent had graduated with a bachelor's degree or higher. This study indicates about 70 percent of the women completed a high school and about 7 percent of the women completed college. Compared with the 1990 census, educational attainment of the women in this study is lower than average Korean women, including Korean-American women, in the United States.

Table 6

English Proficiency of the Respondents

English Proficiency	Speaking		Reading		Writing	
	N	%	N	%	N	%
Fluent	1	1.4	1	1.4	1	1.4
Good	5	6.7	3	4.1	7	9.5
Fair	17	23.0	36	48.6	28	37.8
Poor	44	59.5	30	40.5	31	41.9
Not at all	7	9.4	4	5.4	7	9.4
Total	74	100.0	74	100.0	74	100.0

As indicated in Table 6, only one woman reported fluency in speaking, reading, and writing the English language. The vast majority of the Korean women indicate poor or no ability in speaking the English language. About 46 percent of the women indicate poor or no ability in reading English; about 51 percent of them indicate poor or no ability in writing in the English language. The women's low ability in the English language seems to be related to lack of non-familial contact in the United States. According to Mangiafico's research (1988, 162), only 3 percent of Koreans in the United States speak English fluently. According to the 1990 census, 63.5 percent of Koreans in the United States did not speak English "very well," and 41.1 percent were linguistically isolated.

Table 7

Present Occupations of Respondents' Husbands

Occupation	N	%	Cumulated %
Blue-collar	36	68.0	68.0
White-collar	17	32.0	100.0
Total	53	100.0	

Missing observations=21

The Korean women who reported their husbands' occupations indicated more blue-collar jobs than white-collar jobs as shown in Table 7. The blue-collar jobs include janitor, laundry worker, maintenance worker, mechanic, truck driver, and welder. The white-collar jobs include dental technician, editor, public official, salesman, and other salaried workers. The questionnaire asked the last occupations the women and their husbands held in Korea. Forty-six Korean women gave their husbands' former occupations in Korea rather than their own former occupations. This response apparently is accounted for by the fact that in Korea employment for married women is restricted. In Korea, 37 percent of the women's husbands held blue-collar jobs, such as carpenter and taxi driver, while 54 percent of them held white-collar jobs such as banker, nurse, or teacher. Four of the women's husbands owned sewing businesses in Korea. In contrast to their present occupations in the United States, the women's husbands held more white-collar jobs than blue-collar jobs in Korea. According to Mangiafico (1988, 162-163), major reasons among Koreans for immigration to the United States were for family reunification (50.3%) followed by educational opportunity (43.2%), better employment opportunities (42.8%) and others (17.8%).

Table 8

Comparison of Length of Working Experience in the Apparel Industry and the Present Company

Length of working Experience	the Apparel company		the Present company	
	N	%	N	%
Less than 1 year	1	1.4	19	26.0
1 year- 2 years	17	23.3	27	37.0
3 years- 4 years	17	23.3	11	15.1
5 years- 6 years	15	20.5	6	8.2
7 years- 8 years	3	4.1	4	5.5
9 years-10 years	8	11.0	4	5.5
11 years-15 years	12	16.4	2	2.7
Total	73	100.0	73	100.0

Missing observation=1

In this study, length of working experience in the apparel industry ranges from 5 months to 14 years. The average length of working experience is 5.8 years in the apparel industry and 2.9 years with the present company. The modal length of working experience is 3 years in the industry and one year with the present company. More than 50 percent of the women have more than 5 years of working experience in the apparel industry. More than 60 percent of the women have less than 3 years of working experience in the present company. About 22 percent of the women have more than 5 years working experience in the present company. All of the Korean women in this study are sewers.

Table 9

Respondents' Monthly Income and Total Family Household Income in 1991

Monthly Income	Respondents' Income*		Family Income**	
	N	%	N	%
$ 500 - 999	8	12.1	0	0.0
$ 1,000 - 1,499	26	39.4	0	0.0
$ 1,500 - 1,999	22	33.4	3	5.5
$ 2,000 - 2,499	8	12.1	7	12.7
$ 2,500 - 2,999	1	1.5	11	20.0
$ 3,000 - 3,499	0	0.0	14	25.5
$ 3,500 - 3,999	0	0.0	10	18.2
$ 4,000 - 4,499	1	1.5	5	9.1
$ 4,500 - 4,999	0	0.0	2	3.6
$ 5,000 +	0	0.0	3	5.4
Total	66	100.0	55	100.0

*Missing observations=8
**Missing observations=19

The exact amount of income among the Korean women was difficult to get from the sample group, because their jobs in the apparel industry are seasonal ones where they are paid by the piece. About 95 percent of the women report that they are paid by the piece. Only 5 percent report that they are paid hourly, weekly, or monthly. Therefore, the working women's monthly incomes reported in Table 9 are based on their average income. About 12 percent of the women report monthly individual incomes below $1,000. None of them reports that their family incomes are below $1,500. The modal monthly income categories are $1,000-1,499 for the Korean women and $3,000-3,499 for the Korean married couples. The monthly income distribution of the women ranges from $600-4,000, while the married couples' incomes range from $1,500-5,500. The average monthly individual income of the Korean working women is $1,380, while the average monthly income of the married-couple families is $3,096. The average monthly household income of the married-couple families ($3,147) is slightly higher than all household incomes where women are the primary wage-earners. Multiplying the couples' monthly incomes by 12 indicates that the annual family income of married-couples is $37,152, above the median income of the Southern region ($25,870) of the United States in 1989. However, the family income of the couples is slightly below the median income of married-couple families ($38,664) reported in 1989 by the U.S. Bureau of the Census.

In summary, the majority of the Korean women are married. The modal number of children among them is two. About 44 percent of the women have minor children under 12 years of age, whereas about 23 percent of them have adult children over 18 years of age. Concerning the present occupation of the women's husbands, more blue-collar jobs than white-collar jobs are reported; however, the women's husbands held more white collar jobs than blue collar jobs in Korea. In this study, all of the Korean women are sewers. Their average length of working experience is 5.8 years in the apparel industry and 2.9 years with the present company. The majority of the women are 30 to 49 years of age. All of the women came to the United States between 1974 and 1990. Their average length of residence in the United States is 7.2 years, and the length of time in Dallas is 6.5 years. The majority of the women reported that they "completed high school" in Korea, while more than 95 percent of them have had no education at all in the United States. Only one woman reports fluency in English (in speaking, reading, and writing); the majority report difficulty with the English language.

About 95 percent of the women report that they are paid to work by the piece. The average monthly income is $1,380 for the women, $3,096 for the women and their spouses. The married couple's income is a little less than that of married couples' household income in the United States as reported in 1989 by the U.S. Bureau of the Census. More than half of the women reside in rented houses. Concerning the respondents household composition, more than half indicate a nuclear type of family; 11 percent report a matrifocal family type, and 10 percent an extended family type. Only one woman lives alone.

Familial Roles

One of the reasons the Korean women prefer the apparel jobs is that they can accommodate the apparel jobs to their familial roles. Especially in the case of home sewers, they believe that they can be close to their children. Since the apparel work is paid by the piece, most of the women seem willing to work for a long period of time in order to earn more income. There is no doubt about the women's financial contributions to their families, but on the other hand, there are some questions that arise regarding the time they spend in their familial roles. They have limited time to spend on household work and child care and this creates some dissatisfaction, especially about the time they spend with their children. The generation gap may be widened because of a lack of communication between the women and their children. Among the women, the familial roles seem to be the most important to them with only about one-third reporting a desire to work when their households do not need their financial support. Most of the women have a strong desire to work but see work as temporary, to support their families. Most prefer their familial role to their work role, as would be true for the traditional Korean women. But the characteristics of the women are a little different from those of the traditional Korean married women. The women are working, and most of them live in a nuclear family with two children; their labor-force participation challenges the patriarchal family.

The data provided by the respondents suggest the beginning of a period of change for traditional Korean women. However, it seems too early to mention the women in a feminist perspective. The process of changing gender roles will take time, because such change is closely related to the socialization process in the family. As Mrs. P's case shows, even the family expectations of boys and girls are different. Mrs. P lives with her husband, an 11-year-old son, and a 13-year-old daughter. Mr. P is a salaried worker. Mrs. P is a home sewer, paid $6.50 to $7.00 for each piece for her work. She sews 150 pieces of pre-cut garments every 2 weeks. The yearly family income (husband and wife combined) is about $38,000 to $43,000. About 5 percent of the family's income is spent for clothes, about 15 percent for food, about 25 percent for housing, about 30 percent for saving, and about 25 percent for other needs, including personal expenditure. Mrs. P's family members participate in household work frequently. Mr. P's job is house cleaning; her daughter's job is doing the laundry, while her son's job is not assigned. Mrs. P said, "He is not old enough to do housework, and he is a boy." Mrs. P spends 3 or 4 hours a day in housework and about 10 hours sewing. She does not spend any time just taking care of her children; rather, she always watches her children while she is working at home. Mrs. P grew up in a patriarchal family; therefore, her attitudes come from her background. Most traditional Korean families are male-centered, and males are regarded as more valuable than females. In some cases, baby girls grow up as unwanted children. In the family, sons do not participate in any household chores while daughters are expected to be little helpers for mother. Starting from birth, sons are treated as very special in the family.

In classical times the gentle submission of woman to man was regarded as a virtue in Korean society. Even now, to be a wise mother and a good wife is the most important role for the Korean woman. The role of the married woman is to assist her husband. Usually a woman is portrayed as a subordinate and dependent being, rather than as a creative independent being. Given this patriarchal background, it is understandable that women have different attitudes and sex-role expectations of children. Sex-role behavior is not a result of individual character, rather it is a result of social character. Yoon (1977, 158) pointed out that in traditional patriarchal societies the motive for the development of female resources is to use women's labor, not a concern for women's equality. Although change may be beginning, the Korean family in the United States seems also to be under a patriarchal structure. In order to identify the familial roles among the Korean immigrant women in the apparel industry, 13 questions about the following subjects were asked of the women: willingness to give up working, perceived financial contribution, degree of equality with husband, family members' housework participation, hours spent in housework, degree of familial role satisfaction, child care, the importance of self in the family, and degree of satisfaction with family life. The following data describe the Korean women's familial roles.

Table 10

Respondents' Willingness to Give Up Working, Perceived Financial Contribution, and Acceptance of Subordination to Husbands

	N=74	%	Cumulated %
Willingness to Give Up Working			
Definitely yes	16	21.6	21.6
Probably yes	24	32.4	54.0
Don't know	8	10.9	64.9
Probably no	18	24.3	89.2
Definitely no	8	10.8	100.0
Perceived Financial Contribution			
Definitely yes	46	62.2	62.2
Probably yes	24	32.4	94.6
Don't know	1	1.4	95.9
Probably no	2	2.7	98.6
Definitely no	1	1.4	100.0
Acceptance of Subordination			
Definitely yes	13	17.5	17.5
Probably yes	38	51.3	68.8
Don't know	11	14.9	83.7
Probably no	7	9.5	93.2
Definitely no	5	6.8	100.0

Not surprisingly, more than 50 percent of the Korean women report their willingness to give up their job immediately when their households do not need any financial support, while about 35 percent of them show their desire to continue to work in the apparel industry regardless of need (see Table 10). The women's financial contributions to the household were examined with the following question: "How much of your salary do you contribute to your family's?" The vast majority of the Korean women (95%) say they do not manage their income independently, rather they put their earnings together with their spouses' as family income. The remaining women report that they spend their incomes for saving, food, housing, etc. In this study, more than 90 percent of the Korean women reported that they contribute to their families' economic well-being financially. The Korean women's financial contributions within the family seem to be needed. Only three women report that their work in the apparel industry does not contribute to their families financially (see Table 10).

Mrs. L's case illustrates the Korean women's economic roles within the family. Mrs. L's life in the United States began with a sewing job. Mrs. L, 35 years old, lives with her husband, a 2-year-old and a 10-year-old daughter. She was the breadwinner while her husband received training in a technical school for 6 months. A year later, her family was secure financially. Mrs. L is free from financial pressure. Now, Mr. L is working as a welder. Mrs. L is very satisfied with her husband's job and with his high income; however, even though her family does not need her income, Mrs. L is still working as a sewer. A great reward from her job is to being able to save money. "Since I do not have any financial pressure, to work is just a fun thing. Now, I have a sizable bank account. I believe I am a strong woman psychologically as well as physically. I am very happy." She has worked in the apparel industry for 6 years.

As indicated in Table 10, the majority of the Korean women report that women should definitely or probably have a subordinate position to their husbands in the family. Only 16.3 percent of the women indicate that women should not have a subordinate position in the family. About 15 percent of them did not respond to this question. Regardless of the length of working hours of the Korean women, about 70 percent of them report that they think women should have a subordinate position to their husbands in the family. With one exception, women who work from 31 to 40 hours per week report that women probably or definitely should have a subordinate position to their husbands in the family. None of the women who work from 71 to 80 hours reports that women definitely should have a subordinate position to their husbands.

Table 11

Family Members' Housework Participation, Hours Spent Doing Housework, and Degree of Familiar Role Satisfaction of the Respondents

	$\underline{N}$=74	%	Cumulated %
Housework Participation			
All the time	21	28.8	28.8
Very Often	11	15.1	43.8
Sometimes	35	47.9	91.8
Seldom	6	8.2	100.0
Never	0	0.0	
Hours Spent Per Day Doing Housework			
10+ hours	3	4.1	4.1
7-9 hours	2	2.7	6.8
5-6 hours	14	18.9	25.7
3-4 hours	37	50.0	75.7
Less than 2 hours	18	24.3	100.0
Degree of Familiar Role Satisfaction			
Very satisfied	13	17.5	17.5
Somewhat satisfied	29	39.2	56.7
Don't know	15	20.3	77.0
Somewhat dissatisfied	17	23.0	100.0
Very dissatisfied	0	0.0	

The majority of the Korean women's family members participate in housework as indicated in Table 11. Almost 44 percent of the family members participate in housework all the time or very often. The vast majority of the women indicate some participation by family members in housework. More than 8 percent of the women report that their family members almost never participate in housework, and none say that family members never participate in housework. As shown in Table 11, more than 90 percent of the Korean women spend less than 6 hours per day doing housework. The median hours spent doing housework each day are 4, and the mean hours are 3.9. When the mean hours of 3.9 hours are multiplied by 7 for the mean hours per week, it comes out to 27.3 hours. Compared with McAllister's study (1990) in Australia, which reported 32 hours for the Australian women's household labor per week, it seems that the Korean working women spend fewer hours in household labor than do the Australian working women. The modal hours spent doing housework is 3 to 4 hours per day. Almost 60 percent of the Korean women indicate that they are very or somewhat satisfied with their family roles, while almost 25 percent indicate that they are somewhat dissatisfied with their roles within the family. None of the Korean women indicates that they are very dissatisfied with their roles within the family (see Table 11).

In order to investigate the sources of child care of the Korean women, the following question was asked: "If you have minor children, who takes care of them?" Two major sources of child care are investigated: the women and their husbands, and their children's grandparents. Almost 8 percent of the married Korean women who have minor children report that their children take care of themselves. Almost another 8 percent of the women report their Korean neighbors are a source of child care. In this study, the women do not prefer to use a nursery for child care. Mrs. K, a 41-year-old ex-employee, had the same experience as the majority of the Korean women who do not prefer a nursery as a type of child care. When she came to the United States, she had two children: a 3-year-old son and a one-year-old daughter. Mrs. K described her experiences as follows:

> The term "nursery" was not familiar to me, because in Korea the nursery for child care was not well developed. Frankly speaking, I was afraid to leave my children in a nursery. My children did not understand the English language at that time. Also, I did not trust a nursery center; rather, I preferred an elderly Korean who could take care of my children

only. But it was not convenient for me because I did not have my own car; therefore, I decided to work at home. Then, I did not need to worry about my kids any more. I was a teacher in Korea, but it was a good start to learn the life in the United States. Two years later, I could get my own car; also my husband had his own business. Then I could leave the sewing job. I did not need to stay in the same job anymore. My children were grown up, I saved some money, and I learned the English language.

Table 12

Sources of Child Care and Feeling about Respondents' Time Spent with Children

	$\underline{N}$=74	%	Cumulated %
Sources of Child Care			
Parents	20	52.6	52.6
Grandparents	10	26.3	78.9
Children themselves	3	7.9	86.8
Others	3	7.9	94.7
Nursery	2	5.3	100.0
Feeling about Time Spent with children			
Very satisfied	8	10.8	10.8
Somewhat satisfied	17	23.0	33.8
Don't know	19	25.7	59.5
Somewhat dissatisfied	28	37.8	97.3
Very dissatisfied	2	2.7	100.0

Through the interview with Mrs. K, I was able to realize why the Korean women prefer parents and children's grandparents as the major sources of child care. There are cultural differences between Korea and the United States regarding child care, and a Korean preference for individual care seemed to be the most important factor for determining the sources of child care.

In this study, the vast majority of the Korean married women (95%) report that they spend less than 5 hours a day taking care of their children. One-half of the Korean women spend 2 to 3 hours a day with their children. About 2 percent of the women indicate that they spend 5 to 10 hours caring for their children. Another 2 percent of the women report that they cannot count the time they spend caring for their children because the time is too variable to count. About one percent of the women report that they always take care of their children.

The Korean married women with children indicate that they are more dissatisfied than satisfied with the time spent with their children. About 34 percent of the women report that they are very or somewhat satisfied, while about 40 percent of them report that they are somewhat or very dissatisfied regarding time spent with their children (see Table 12). Mrs. R's case shows an immigrant working mother's feeling about the time spent with their children.

> I am ashamed of my illiteracy of the English language. I used to say I came to the United States for my children's better education and their bright future. But frankly speaking, I have not spent enough time with them. I spend more time working. I thought it was the best way for them. I mean, I thought financial support was a more important factor than anything else. I have a 16-year-old boy and a 12-year-old girl. I came to the United States in 1977, when my son was 2 years old. After my son entered junior high school, I realized we had some gap between us. The gap was getting wider and wider because of a lack of communication. I should have learned the English language or I should have taught Korean language to my children, but I did not do either. Now, I wonder why I came to the United States. For my children? Or for myself?

As data reported in Table 6 indicate, the majority of the Korean women have difficulty with the English language. In addition, the vast majority were educated in Korea (See Table 5), while their children have been educated in the United States. Therefore, cultural and educational experiences of the parents' generation and the children's generation are very different. To overcome a conflict between parents and children, their mutual understanding and willingness to learn different cultures seem to be very important.

Only a quarter of the Korean women in this study report some leisure activities, such as attending church services, watching Korean video tapes, shopping, or having dinner in a restaurant. Because of the busy schedule of the working women, their leisure activities and kinship obligations seem to be limited and individualistic. Only one-third of the Korean women report spending time with their relatives. It is assumed that the majority of the women do not live near their relatives. The Korean women's major kinship relationships are phone calls, family dinners, birthday parties, and holiday parties.

Table 13

Respondents' Importance in the Family and Degree of Satisfaction with Family Life

	$\underline{N}$	%	Cumulated %
Importance of respondent			
Very important	49	66.2	66.2
Somewhat important	22	29.7	95.9
Don't know	2	2.7	98.6
Somewhat unimportant	1	1.4	100.0
Very unimportant	0	0.0	
Degree of Satisfaction with Family Life			
Very satisfied	9	12.2	12.2
Somewhat satisfied	40	54.1	66.2
Don't know	9	12.2	78.4
Somewhat dissatisfied	15	20.3	98.6
Very dissatisfied	1	1.4	100.0

In this study, the majority of the Korean women consider themselves to be very or somewhat important in their families. Only one woman considers herself somewhat unimportant in her family. None of the women considers herself very unimportant (see Table 13). The high proportion of the women's perception of their importance in the family demonstrates their preference for familial roles. Almost two-thirds of the Korean women show satisfaction with family life. About one-fifth of the women report that they are somewhat dissatisfied with their family lives. In this study, only one Korean woman indicates that she is very dissatisfied with her family life (see Table 13).

In summary, more than 90 percent of the Korean women report that their work in the apparel industry has contributed to their family financially. The vast majority (91.8%) of the women indicate some participation by their family members in housework. More than 90 percent of the women spend fewer than 6 hours per day doing housework. The modal daily hours spent doing housework is 3 to 4. Two major sources of child care for the women are the women themselves, their husbands, and their children's grandparents. Regarding feelings about time spent with their children, about 34 percent of the women show some degree of satisfaction, while about 40 percent of them indicate some degree of dissatisfaction. Almost 60 percent of the women show some degree of satisfaction with their familial roles. Regardless of the length of working hours of the women, about 70 percent of them indicate that women should have a subordinate position to their husbands in the family. Almost 70 percent of the women indicate their satisfaction with their family life. More than 95 percent of the women consider themselves as important persons in their families.

Work Roles

The Korean women work in the apparel industry an average of 53.7 hours per week. In a peak season, the working hours can be even longer than the average working hours. The women's long working hours in the apparel industry well reflect their work roles and also reflect their strong desire to achieve financial success in the United States. More than one-third of the women stated their desire to continue to work in the apparel industry regardless of need. The women's labor-force participation, on the one hand, supports their families' well-being. On the other hand, the labor-force participation reflects their wish to be financially independent. The women do not want to reach their financial success simply through their husbands' economic activities. Their financial contributions seem to be a very important to the Korean immigrant family, not only in the beginning stage, but also in the later, more settled stage. With the women's willingness to work in the apparel industry, the Korean immigrant family is able to attain an early condition of stability in the United States (see p. 57 Mrs. L's case).

Some problematic factors exist for workers in the apparel industry. Ventilation is poor. There is no resting place. A lot of physical stress comes from long working hours as well as psychological stress from the demands of meeting deadlines. In addition, the pay per garment is low and constant, while the cost of living is rising. These conditions seem to be contributing factors to the women's working hours getting longer and longer. In addition, despite the women's intensive work participation, most do not feel themselves to be an important force in the apparel industry, reflecting their alienation from the work in which they participate and supporting Marx's concept of alienation from labor. Like most immigrants in the past, most of the women do not consider the apparel industry as a future career for their children.

In order to investigate work roles among the Korean immigrant women in the apparel industry, 26 questions about the following subjects were asked of the participants: job information, selection of a company, working conditions, sense of accomplishment, attitude toward working women, satisfaction with present employer, job benefits, desire to stay in the apparel industry, gender advantages, equality of position, income satisfaction, preference for apparel industry as children's future employment, advantages and/or disadvantages of the job, and problems in the apparel company. The following is helpful in describing the Korean women's work roles.

Most of the women learned their job skills from a neighbor, a friend, a relative, another sewing company, from self-practice, or from an apparel institution in Korea. Excerpts from in-depth interviews represent how the Korean women enter the apparel industry. For example, Mrs. K, ex-employee, described her reason for choosing the sewing job as follows: 1) the lack of knowledge of the English language, 2) mistrust of the child-care facilities, and 3) lack of experience about life in the United States. Mrs. K, who had 2 years working experience in the garment industry, came to the United States in the early 1980s. Her first job in the United States was to put buttons on garments in a garment company. With that job, she began to learn how to sew. A month later, she could sew a simple part, such as a belt. Three months later, she began working as a sewer and could complete a simple garment, such as a shirt. A year later, she could sew all kinds of garments. Even though her financial contribution to her family was not great, she began to learn about the reality of life in the United States. Mrs. K describes the sewing job as "the very first step for the immigrants." Now she has a small sandwich shop business.

The case of Mrs. P (see also p. 54), who has been working in the apparel industry for 5 years, is a little different. To be a sewer she practiced sewing at home for almost 3 months. A year later, Mrs. P's sewing skill was recognized as excellent. Now she is sewing a quality garment and is paid for high price. Her dream is to be self-employed as an owner of an alterations shop.

Table 14

Most Important Factor for the Respondents' in Selecting an Employer

Important Factor	$\underline{N}$	%	Cumulated %
Salary	38	52.8	52.8
Working conditions	12	16.7	69.5
Job position	10	13.9	83.4
Employer	9	12.5	95.9
Location	3	4.1	100.0
Total		72	100.0

Missing observations=2

Salary is cited as the most important factor when the Korean working women choose a company with which to work. Other factors are listed as follows: working conditions, the type of job, employer, and location (see Table 14). It shows clearly the women's economic motivation is the first factor considered in deciding to work.

Table 15

Respondents' Working Hours Per Week and Working Place

	N	%	Cumulated %
Working Hours*			
Less than 10 hours	1	1.4	1.4
31-40 hours	12	17.4	18.8
41-50 hours	18	26.1	44.9
51-60 hours	26	37.7	82.6
61-70 hours	8	11.6	94.2
71-80 hours	4	5.8	100.0
Working Place			
Home	18	24.3	24.3
Home and company	28	37.8	62.1
Company	28	37.9	100.0

*Missing observations=5

More than 80 percent of the Korean women report that they work more than 40 hours per week, as indicated in Table 15. The median working hours are 55, and the mean hours are 53.7 per week. Almost 30 percent of the women work mornings and afternoons; about 15 percent of them work from early morning to evening (including 10.8 percent that work late at night); and about 12 percent of them work from morning to evening. Almost 38 percent of the women work on the premises of their companies; about 38 percent of them work in both the home and the business; and about 24 percent of them work in their homes only (see Table 15). The majority of the women (82.4%) indicate that they hold the same job now as in the beginning of their work in the garment industry. Presumably the rest of the Korean women (16.2%) started in "*shiage*" (see p. 43) and were promoted to a sewer position later.

Table 16

Respondents' Degree of the Perceived Importance in the Present Company

Degree of the Importance	N	%	Cumulated %
Very important	7	9.5	9.5
Moderately important	22	29.7	39.2
Don't know	19	25.7	64.9
A little important	18	24.3	89.2
Not at all	8	10.8	100.0
Total	74	100.0	

As shown in Table 16, only about 40 percent of the Korean women report that their positions are very or moderately important in the present company while about 35 percent of them indicate that their positions are of little or no importance. A little more than a quarter of the women show indifference toward the present job.

Table 17

Respondents' Sense of Accomplishment on the Job

Sense of Accomplishment	N	%	Cumulated %
Definitely yes	4	5.4	5.4
Probably yes	30	40.5	45.9
Don't know	7	9.5	55.4
Probably not	25	33.0	89.2
Definitely not	8	10.8	100.0
Total	74	100.0	

To identify the women's sense of accomplishment on the present job, the following question was asked: "How much satisfaction do you get from the company you work for?" As Table 18 shows, about 46 percent of the women indicate some positive degree of accomplishment (definitely or probably), while about 44 percent of them report some negative degree of accomplishment (probably or definitely).

Table 18

Perception of People's Attitude Toward Working Women

People's Attitude	N	%	Cumulated %
Very positively	16	21.6	21.6
Somewhat positively	34	45.9	67.5
Don't know	14	19.0	86.5
Somewhat negatively	10	13.5	100.0
Very negatively	0	0.0	
Total	74	100.0	

About 68 percent of the Korean working women indicate that they think that people have a very or somewhat positive feelings toward working women in general, while about 14 percent of them think people have somewhat negative feelings about working women. None of the Korean women indicates that she feels that people have a very negative feeling toward working women (see Table 18).

Table 19

Respondents' Feeling About the Present Working Conditions and Degree of Satisfaction with the Present Company

	N=74	%	Cumulated %
Feeling about the working conditions			
Very satisfied	1	1.4	1.4
Somewhat satisfied	39	52.6	54.0
Don't know	8	10.8	68.8
Somewhat dissatisfied	23	31.1	95.9
Very dissatisfied	3	4.1	100.0
Degree of satisfaction			
A great deal	5	6.8	6.8
Moderate	37	50.0	56.8
Don't know	7	9.4	66.2
A little	18	24.3	90.5
Not at all	7	9.5	100.0

Regarding their present working conditions, 54 percent of the Korean women show some degree of satisfaction (very or somewhat) with their present working conditions, while about 35 percent of them report some degree of dissatisfaction (very or somewhat). More than half of the Korean women indicate their satisfaction with the present company in some degree (including a great deal of satisfaction). About 34 percent of the women show their dissatisfaction with the present company and among those about 10 percent report that they are not at all satisfied in the present company (see Table 19).

Table 20

Frequency of Job Change Among the Respondents
from the Beginning to Now

Frequency	N	%	Cumulated %
None	16	21.6	21.6
1- 2	19	25.6	47.2
3- 4	25	33.7	80.9
5- 6	8	10.9	91.8
7- 8	1	1.4	93.2
9-10	1	1.4	94.6
Don't know	4	5.4	100.0
Total	74	100.0	

The frequency of job turnover among the Korean women from the beginning to the present ranged from none to 10 times, as indicated in Table 20. The median and mean job changes are 2.5. Since the mean working years are 5.8 years (see Table 8), the mean job changes per year are .43.

Table 21

Perceived Interpersonal Relationship Between
Employee and Employer

Good Relationship	N	%	Cumulated %
Definitely yes	18	24.3	24.3
Probably yes	38	51.4	75.7
Don't know	12	16.2	91.9
Probably not	6	8.1	100.0
Definitely not	0	0.0	
Total	74	100.0	

The majority of the Korean women report that in general they have a good relationship with their employers. This is much higher number than those expressing satisfaction about their present working conditions. It seems the women are so grateful to their employers, who provide them jobs, that they feel they cannot complain. The low rate of job turnover in the previous Table 20 supports the women's good relationships with their employers. Only 8 percent of the women indicate that they do not have a good relationship with their employers. None indicated a definitely bad relationship with her employer (see Table 21).

Almost 9 percent of the Korean women indicate that the company provides lunch for employees. However, none of the apparel companies in this study has a sick-leave benefit. As shown in Table 22, the

Table 22

Possession of Medical Insurance of the Respondents

Holding Medical Insurance	N	%	Cumulated %
Yes	20	27.0	27.0
No	54	73.0	100.0
Total	74	100.0	

majority of the Korean women report that they do not have medical insurance. Only 27 percent of the women have medical insurance.

About 42 percent of the women responded to a question about the length of time they desire to stay in the apparel industry, and 45 percent indicated a desire to leave the industry immediately. More than 35 percent of the women want to stay in the apparel industry as long as they remain physically able to work; 13 percent of them wish to stay until their children can support themselves; and 6.5 percent of them want to stay until they accumulate capital for their own businesses.

Korean Immigrant Women In The Dallas Apparel Industry 73

To identify gender equality in the present company, the following questions were asked: "Do you think males get more advantages than females in the present company? If your answer is yes, what kind of advantages do males have in the present company?" "Do you think women should have less important positions than men at the workplace?" "Do you think males get better positions than females in the present company?" The vast majority of the Korean women (86.5%) indicate males do not get more advantages than females in the present company. Only about 14 percent report that males get advantages in terms of their physical strength.

Regarding the difference between the sexes in the importance of work positions, about 16 percent of the Korean women report women should definitely (10.8%) or probably (5.8%) have less important positions than men, while about 45 percent of them indicate women should probably (43.2%) or definitely (1.4%) not have less important positions. The vast majority of the Korean women (82.4%) report that males probably (47.3%) or definitely (35.1%) do not get better positions than females in the present company, while about 15 percent of them indicate that males probably (8.1%) get better positions than females. None of the Korean women indicates that males definitely get better positions than females in the present company. In general, the apparel industry is perceived as providing equal opportunity regardless of sex.

Table 23

Respondents' Sense that Income is Equitable for Educational Level

Sense to Income Equity	N	%	Cumulated %
Definitely yes	4	5.4	5.4
Probably yes	18	24.3	29.7
Don't know	11	14.9	44.6
Probably not	31	41.9	86.5
Definitely not	10	13.5	100.0
Total	74	100.0	

As indicated in Table 23, about 30 percent of the Korean women report that their incomes are reasonable, given their educational levels. About 55 percent of them indicate that their incomes are not reasonable in some respects. The women's income dissatisfaction demonstrates the nature of the garment industry which is overrepresented by female workers with a low wage.

Table 24

Respondents' Preference of the Apparel Industry as Their Children's Future Working Area

Respondents' Preference	N	%	Cumulated %
Definitely yes	0	0.0	0.0
Probably yes	3	4.1	4.1
Don't know	6	8.1	12.2
Probably not	18	24.3	36.5
Definitely not	47	63.5	100.0
Total	74	100.0	

The vast majority of the Korean women indicate that they do not prefer the apparel industry as a place for their children to work. Only 4 percent of the women show some degree of preference (probably) for the apparel industry as their children's future workplace (see Table 24). In the previous data (Table 19) the Korean women report some degree of satisfaction with the present working conditions as well as with the present company, suggesting that even though the women have some degree of satisfaction in the apparel industry, it is the satisfaction of the first generation of immigrants. Their expectations are different, however, for their children. Unlike their children, who have been educated in the United States, most of the women were educated in Korea and, therefore, have limited knowledge of the English language. In addition, they lack job marketability in the United States.

Mrs. R's case represents why the women do not prefer the apparel industry as their children's future working area. Mrs. R, 38 years old, is satisfied to live in the United States because she can work even though she is working in an apparel company. When she was in Korea, she worked as a secretary in a large company. But when she married, she had to leave the company against her will. The early retirement from employment for marriage was applicable to most Korean career women, especially in the 1970s when Mrs. R left Korea. Therefore, she is very satisfied that she can work in the United States. Mrs. R said:

> After I lost the job, I tried to search out another job. It was almost impossible. A company tried to take advantage of my status as a married woman. The company offered me almost half of my previous income. It was miserable. Then I gave up to get a new job.

She lives with her husband, a 16-year-old son, and a 12-year-old daughter. When I asked her preference about the apparel industry as her children's future work area, Mrs. R showed her strong negative feeling about the industry. She said:

> ... there is no reason for my children to work in the apparel industry. My children have been educated in the United States. I have never been in doubt about their bright future. They will get a good job, I mean, a professional job. The life of my children's generation should be different from their parents' generation, I believe. I think I am overqualified to work in the apparel company. I do not mean that educated people cannot work in the apparel industry. I cannot complain because I have not been educated in the United States.

Mrs. R's case seems to be typical of the Korean immigrant's family in the United States. Most Korean immigrants have a strong desire to educate their children as well as a strong wish to achieve their goals through their children.

In order to investigate the advantages and/or disadvantages and any problems of working in the apparel industry, the following open-ended questions were asked: "What are the advantages and/or disadvantages of working in the apparel industry?" "Do you have any problems working in this apparel company?" The great advantage of working in the apparel industry was identified as flexibility of working hours (43%). Along with working in the apparel company, workers can do household work, especially taking care of their children. However, the following disadvantages and problems were also reported by the Korean women: 1) a low unit pay for garments (26%); 2) long working hours (26%); 3) bad ventilation (14%); 4) a lack of exercise (7%); 5) no opportunity for learning the life of the United States, including learning the English language (7%); 6) no resting place (5%); 7) bad working conditions (5%); 8) excessive physical labor (5%); 9) no insurance (4%); 10) a lot of noise (4%); and 11) instability of income (4%).

Excerpts from in-depth interviews provide more concerning the advantages and/or disadvantages of working in the apparel industry. For example, Mrs. P, who is a home sewer, points out that the great advantage of her sewing job is the flexibility of working hours. In addition, she can take care of her children while she works. In addition to the advantages of working in the apparel industry, the employees pointed out some problems. For example, there is a peak season and an off season; therefore, income is not stable. Workplaces are not equipped with proper ventilation. There is a lot of physical and psychological pressure, and workers must meet deadlines. Especially in peak season, working hours are extremely long; to spend an entire night working is not unusual.

Employers also have problems with the management of garment companies. The unit pay for garments is very low and relatively constant, while a designed garment may be complex to sew. Compared to 10 years ago, the pay per garment is almost the same. Mr. B who is the owner of a garment company, describes the garment job as "legal slavery." He said, "I am an owner in this company, but I do not think I am an owner here." He pointed out his subordinate relationship as a subcontractor to a main company. "If the main company does not provide previously cut garments, there is no way to remain in this business." Therefore, insecurity in this business is visible. Mr. B also pointed out the high rate of turnover among employees. According to Mr. B, one of the reasons the garment industry cannot give benefits to the employees is the high rate of turnover. The high rate of turnover affects the apparel industry in terms of managing a working schedule as well as building up credit from main companies. Mr. B emphasized the importance of mutual understanding, cooperation, and a work ethic between employees and employers in order to survive in this business.

When I visited apparel companies to collect data, some companies had fewer than five employees present. A working woman employee said it was off season. It was in the middle of July in 1991. Some of the women said the business decline was due to an economic depression. "Especially a high unit price of garments is closely related to economic conditions. This company deals with only a costly garment. We cannot survive with a cheap unit price on garments." The high unit pay for garments during this period of economic recession seems to be one reason for a bad season. Another reason for the apparel industry's off season seems to be excessive competition among companies. Subcontractors' business success seems to be totally dependent on main contractors' orders. If the main company encourages competition among subcontractors, the unit pay for garments will become lower and lower. This condition can be explained by Marx's (1967) concept of capitalist exploitation in the difference between the value of labor power and value created by labor. It is difficult for subcontractors to succeed in this business, whether they win or lose in the competition. Mr. Lee, president of the Korean Texas Garment Contractor's Association, stated that for 10 years in the apparel industry, only about three or four companies have succeeded in this business, suggesting how difficult it is to survive in the apparel industry.

I conducted a complete observation of two apparel companies. The first one had separate working rooms for machine sewing and for the other jobs such as handsewing, making button holes, picking threads, trimming, ironing, folding, and packing. This apparel company had been open for 10 years. It is located in a warehouse area in Garland. The observation was made in April of 1991. I stayed in the company for about 2 hours, from 11:00 a.m. to 1:00 p.m. The main job of the company was to sew pre-cut pieces of women's garments. There were about 15 sewing machines in the sewing room. Six Korean women were working there. The women seemed to be between the ages of 30 and 40. Even though the room was not crowded, noise was excessive. The employer's wife, male manager, and about ten Mexicans, or Mexican-Americans, were working in another room. This room was about 3 times bigger than the sewing room but was crammed with stacked women's garments. Two doors on the opposite sides of the room were open, but the air in the room was not fresh; the room was filled with dust and threads from garments. While the employer's wife was sewing, she also supervised employees. The manager inspected sewed garments for packing. Mexican or Mexican-American women worked as handsewers, buttonholers, and thread cleaners. The ironing was done by a male Mexican worker. During the lunch break, on a sunny day, some of the Mexican women squatted down or stood up outside the building. The women appeared to be in their early 20s.

They were eating snacks or chatting with their fellow workers. The company had a dining room with a dining table for six persons, a two-door, large size refrigerator and kitchen cabinets and sink. It looked clean. The dining room seemed also to be used as a resting area because there was no separate resting area. Outside the dining room, there was a vending machine for drinks. This company's working conditions looked better than other companies in terms of space for working and cleanliness in the dining room. Although the company still had the problems of dust and noise, it may be an example of one of the "nice places" to work in the apparel industry.

The second company I visited was in Irving where there many Korean small businesses are concentrated. This company had a large working room. Almost 30 people were working. It was very crowded and excessively noisy. Smells from the fabrics made my head ache. The company had a small lounge with a round table for four persons. This was a typical example of the apparel industry. Most of the companies have no windows or small-sized windows. The noise of sewing machines is excessive in a small working area. I did not find any resting areas, except a small lounge or dining room. Working conditions at home seemed to be better than in the companies, in terms of cleanliness and noise.

I visited the homes of two sewers during March and April of 1991. One home sewer's house (condominium) was located in a middle-class neighborhood in Richardson, Texas. The sewer's and her husband's monthly incomes were more than $5,000. She had a work room in her house. The house was very clean. There was a sewing machine in the working room. The room was filled with pre-cut pieces of garments and already-sewn garments. I interviewed the home sewer for almost 2 hours. During the time, the interview was interrupted several times by her 2-year-old daughter.

Another home sewer's rented house was located in Dallas. Monthly earnings of the sewer and her husband were more than $3,500. She also had a work room in her house. There was a sewing machine, a television set, and a radio in the room. The room was very well organized and clean. I also conducted an in-depth interview with the sewer while she was working. Once the sewing machine was working, we were not able to communicate with each other because of the noise. The sewer had to stop the machine to listen and answer my questions. Both of the informants whose homes were visited have more than 5 years working experience in the apparel industry, and they have well-organized work rooms at home. Their work rooms are clean, but they also do not have any ventilation. The informants were satisfied with their working conditions and seemingly were not aware of the necessity for ventilation for their family members' health. But Mrs. K, ex-employee in the apparel industry, had a different experience. When Mrs. K worked as a home sewer about 10 years ago, she worked in the living room of her house for 2 years. She lived in a two-bedroom apartment. Most of the residents of the apartment were African-American, Mexicans, and Asians. She had a 3-year-old boy and a one-year-old daughter at that time. She could not afford three bedrooms. She rented a sewing machine from a Korean apparel company. To work at home was convenient for her; however, she always felt sorry for her family because of dust and threads from garments. She was not able to keep her house clean. All the family members suffered from noise and dust which she saw as typical for a home sewer's working conditions. She complained the necessity for some ventilation for health.

In summary, salary is indicated as the most important factor for the Korean women's choice of a company. More than 80 percent of the women work more than 40 hours per week. However, only about 40 percent of them report that their positions are very or moderately important in the present company. Concerning the women's sense of accomplishment in the present job, less than half of them have some positive degree of accomplishment. A little more than half of the women show some degree of satisfaction about their present working conditions and their present company. The median and mean frequency of turnover among these women are 2.5 times. The majority of the women (75.7%) have a good relationship with their employers. None of the apparel companies in this study has a sick-leave benefit and the majority of the women (73%) do not have medical insurance. About 45 percent of the women wish to leave the apparel industry immediately. The vast majority (86.5%) indicate that males do not get more advantage than females in the present company. Concerning the women's satisfaction with their present incomes, given their educational levels, only 30 percent of the women report that their incomes are reasonable. The vast majority of the women (89.8%) do not prefer the apparel industry for their children's future work.

Social Roles

Korean married women do not want to financially dependent on their husbands completely. Before they came to the United States, they already had a strong desire to achieve financial success for their families. Since they had an ambition to achieve in the United States, even their hard lives here have not caused them to give up their goals. To make successful lives in the United States, the women did not hesitate to participate in the labor force. Their role in making an financial contribution to the family is not questioned. However, many of the women indicate their feeling that domestic labor is a woman's natural role, and although they work long hours in the apparel industry, many of them accept the man's official role as breadwinner and the woman's role as housekeeper.

In order to assess the social roles among the Korean immigrant women, 12 questions about the following subjects were asked: perceived social class, aims to achieve in the United States, general feeling about working women, perception of women's present status in the family as well as the perceived importance in society, contribution to the Korean-American community, success in achieving goals in the United States, and their happiest time in the United States. The following data describe some of the Korean women's social roles.

The majority of the Korean women perceived themselves as middle class in the United States. In Korea, more than 80 percent of Koreans consider themselves as middle class. Compared with their native country, fewer Korean people in the United States indicate themselves as middle class. About 20 percent of the women report themselves as lower class. About another 20 percent of them did not indicate their perceptions of social class. None of the women indicated their perceived social class as upper class (see Table 25). As shown in Table 25, about 41 percent of the women report that their present living conditions are definitely or probably better than in Korea, while about 49 percent of them indicate that their living conditions in Korea were definitely or probably better than in the United States. The questionnaire asked what the Korean women hoped to achieve by coming to the United States. The women's two major hopes are identified as a better education for their children and financial stability for their families.

Table 25

Respondents' Perceived Social Class in the United States and Comparison of Living Conditions in the United States and in Korea

	N=74	%	Cumulated %
Perceived Social Class			
Upper class	0	0.0	0.0
Middle class	44	59.4	59.4
Lower class	15	20.3	79.7
Don't know	15	20.3	100.0
Perception of Better Living Conditions			
Definitely better	2	2.7	2.7
Probably better	28	37.8	40.5
Don't know	8	10.8	51.4
Probably worse	28	37.8	89.2
Definitely worse	8	10.8	100.0

Table 26

Respondents' Degree of Acceptance of Domestic Labor as a Woman's Natural Role

Degree of Acceptance	N	%	Cumulated %
Definitely yes	19	25.7	25.7
Probably yes	41	55.3	81.0
Don't know	5	6.8	87.8
Probably not	3	4.1	91.9
Definitely not	6	8.1	100.0
Total	74	100.0	

The vast majority of the Korean women seem to accept domestic labor as a woman's natural role. Only 12 percent of the women report that they do not agree that domestic labor is a woman's natural role (see Table 26). The following interviews reflect the perception of woman's natural role. Mrs. M, 45 years old, believes males have advantages over females in terms of intelligence and physical strength in the workplace. While Mrs. O insists that females have advantages over males because sewing is a woman's job, Mrs. M and Mrs. O have somewhat different notions of gender ability in familial roles. Mrs. M, whose husband is a salaried worker, thinks women should have a subordinate position to their husbands' in the family. She is very satisfied with her husband's position as head-of-family and her position as a supporter for her husband. "I think domestic labor is a woman's natural role." She also said "to be loved by my husband is one of the most important things in my marriage." Even though Mrs. M feels somewhat dissatisfied about women's present status in the family as well as in our society, she said:

> Discrimination against women is acceptable in Korean society, because women always have a hard time to maintain careers after they are married. I think marriage is a more important to a woman than her

career. A woman should follow her husband.

Mrs. O, 29 years old, said:

I think to keep order within the family someone has to have more power than the other. But I do not think my husband should have all of control over the family. My husband and I have powers in different areas. In my family, my husband has more power to make any decision outside the family, while I have power inside the family. Domestic labor, of course, is a woman's natural role, I think. I am a working woman, but I never think I am a breadwinner in my family. My income is just a secondary source of income for my family. My main role is to raise children and to do household work.

Mrs. M's family seems to be a traditional, patriarchal Korean family, while Mrs. O's family seems to be more egalitarian. Mrs. O's husband is self-employed. Even though Mrs. O realizes a gender inequality within the family as well as in our society, she tries to accept it as a normal situation.

Table 27

Cross Tabulation of Respondents' Degree of Acceptance of Domestic Labor as a Woman's Natural Role, by Respondent's Working Hours Per Week

Degree of Acceptance	Working Hours Per Week					Total (%)
	31-40 $\underline{N}$	41-50 $\underline{N}$	51-60 $\underline{N}$	61-70 $\underline{N}$	71-80 $\underline{N}$	
Definitely yes	5	3	6	2	1	17 (25.0)
Probably yes	6	11	13	5	3	38 (55.9)
Don't know		2	1	1		4 (5.9)
Probably not	1		2			3 (4.4)
Definitely not		2	3	1		6 (8.8)
Total (%)	12 (17.6)	18 (26.5)	25 (36.8)	9 (13.2)	4 (5.9)	68 (100.0)

Missing observations=6

Despite the Korean women's long working hours, more than 80 percent of them report that a woman's natural role is as domestic laborer (see Table 27). It shows the women's double burdens from employment and the traditional household work.

Table 28

Respondents' Conception of Man's Role as Breadwinner vs. Woman's Role as Housekeeper

Degree of Acceptance	N	%	Cumulated %
Definitely yes	12	16.2	16.2
Probably yes	31	41.9	58.1
Don't know	6	8.1	66.2
Probably not	17	23.0	89.2
Definitely not	8	10.8	100.0
Total	74	100.0	

Almost 60 percent of the Korean women report their acceptance of the man's role as breadwinner and the woman's role as housekeeper, while almost 35 percent of them do not accept the gender roles, as indicated in Table 28. It is assumed that the latter group tend to put emphasis on less traditional roles.

Table 29

Cross Tabulation of Respondents' Conception of Man's Role as Breadwinner vs. Woman's Role as Housekeeper, by Respondents' Working Hours Per Week

Degree of Acceptance	Working Hours Per Week					Total (%)
	31-40 $\underline{N}$	41-50 $\underline{N}$	51-60 $\underline{N}$	61-70 $\underline{N}$	71-80 $\underline{N}$	
Definitely yes	4	1	5	1		11 (16.2)
Probably yes	3	8	10	5	3	29 (42.6)
Don't know	1	3	1			5 (7.4)
Probably not	4	3	6	1	1	15 (22.1)
Definitely not		3	3	3		8 (11.8)
Total (%)	12 (17.6)	18 (26.5)	25 (36.8)	9 (13.2)	4 (5.9)	68 (100.0)

Missing observations=4

As shown in Table 29, even though more than 80 percent of the Korean women's working hours exceed 40 per week, almost 60 percent of them report their acceptance of the man's role as a breadwinner and the woman's as a housekeeper and a child rearer.

The questionnaire asked how the women feel about women working in general. The vast majority (87.7%) feel very positively (19.2%) or somewhat positively (68.5%) about women working in general, while about 6 percent of them feel somewhat negatively. Only one Korean woman feels very negatively about women working in general.

Table 30

Respondents' Sense of Income Equality Compared to Men Who Have the Same Job Capacity

Sense of Equality	N	%	Cumulated %
Definitely yes	43	58.1	58.1
Probably yes	20	27.0	85.1
Don't know	6	8.1	93.2
Probably not	5	6.8	100.0
Definitely not	0	0.0	
Total	74	100.0	

The vast majority of the women indicate that women should receive wages definitely or probably equal to those given men in the same job capacity, while only 6.8 percent of them feel that women probably should not receive equal wages with men (see Table 30). It reflects the majority of the women's perspective of gender equality which is not based on the system of patriarchy but on the quality of work.

Table 31

Respondents' Perception of Women's Status in the Family as well as in Society

Respondent's Feeling	N	%	Cumulated %
Very positively	3	4.1	4.1
Somewhat positively	36	48.6	52.7
Don't know	2	2.7	55.4
Somewhat negatively	28	37.8	93.2
Very negatively	5	6.8	100.0
Total	74	100.0	

About 53 percent of the women report that they feel very or somewhat positively regarding women's present status in the family as well as in society, while about 45 percent of them indicate that they feel somewhat negatively or very negatively. Even though a little more than half of the women show their positive feelings about women's present status, a little less than half of them still show their negative feelings (see Table 31).

Table 32

Perceived Importance of Self in Society Among the Respondents

Perceived Importance	N	%	Cumulated %
Very important	10	13.5	13.5
Somewhat important	28	37.8	51.3
Don't know	29	39.2	90.5
Somewhat unimportant	6	8.1	98.6
Very unimportant	1	1.4	100.0
Total	74	100.0	

More than half of the women indicate that they perceive themselves very or somewhat important in society, while about 10 percent of them report that they perceive themselves to be somewhat or very unimportant. One respondent feels herself very unimportant in society. Almost 40 percent of the women did not respond to the question about perceived importance of self in society (see Table 32). It is assumed that the women have never considered themselves to be important in society or thought about their importance in society because of their lack of social interest.

Table 33

Comparison of Perceived Importance of Self in the Family, in the Workplace, and in Society

Perceived Importance	Family %	Work %	Society %
Very important	66.2	9.5	13.5
Somewhat important	29.7	29.7	37.8
Don't know	2.7	25.7	39.2
Somewhat unimportant	1.4	24.3	8.1
Very unimportant	0.0	0.8	1.4
Total (%)	100.0	100.0	100.0

Concerning the Korean women's perceived importance of self in the family, in the workplace, and in society, about 96 percent report that they perceive themselves as very or somewhat important in the family, followed by about 51 percent who report themselves as important in society, and about 40 percent who see themselves as important in their workplace (see Table 33).

Table 34

Respondents' Degree of Contribution to the Korean-American Community

Agree to Contribution	N	%	Cumulated %
Definitely yes	4	5.4	5.4
Probably yes	23	31.1	36.5
Don't know	17	23.0	59.5
Probably not	25	33.7	93.2
Definitely not	5	6.8	100.0
Total	74	100.0	

As indicated in Table 34, about 37 percent of the women report that they definitely or probably contribute to the Korean-American community, while about 40 percent of them indicate that they probably or definitely do not contribute. It is assumed that more than half of the women have not yet attained sufficient stability financially, psychologically, and socially to pay attention to the Korean-American community. Or they may have little interest in the Korean-American community.

Table 35

Success in Achieving Goals in the United States of Respondents

Degree of Success	N	%	Cumulated %
Very successful	2	2.7	2.7
Moderately successful	11	14.9	17.6
Don't know	22	29.7	47.3
Little successful	27	36.5	83.8
Not at all successful	12	16.2	100.0
Total	74	100.0	

Only 17.6 percent of the Korean women report that they have achieved their goals very successfully or moderately successfully, while more than half of them indicate little or no success as indicated in Table 35. About 30 percent of the women did not answer the question. Even though the women may not have reached their goals yet, other data suggest a positive belief that they will achieve their goals successfully in the United States. About 85 percent of them report a belief in a bright future in the United States. When asked: "What has been the happiest time in your American life?" most of them said the happiest time was when their children make good grades.

In summary, almost 60 percent of the women perceive themselves as middle class. By coming to the United States, they hope to provide a better education for their children and to achieve financial stability for their families. Regarding living conditions in the United States, compared with their native country of Korea, about 41 percent of the women indicate that their present living conditions are better than the living conditions in Korea, while about 50 percent of them report that their living conditions were better in Korea than in the United States. Even though more than 80 percent of the women work more than 40 hours per week, almost 60 percent of them indicate their perception of the man as breadwinner and of the woman as housekeeper and child rearer. Almost 90 percent of the women have positive feelings concerning women working in general. A little more than half of the women feel positively about women's present status in the family and in society, while fewer than half of them feel negatively about it. The women perceive their roles in the family to be most important, followed by other roles in society, and, last, in the workplace.

Perceived Health and Well-Being

Although the working conditions of the Korean women can be harmful for their health, only 27 percent have medical insurance. Health problems with no health care could result from their long working hours. The majority of the women's present health conditions are reported as good and half of them worry about future illnesses. In order to examine the perceived health and well-being among the Korean women in the apparel industry, eight questions about the following subjects were asked of the Korean women: a self-rating of health, any illnesses, worry about future illness, the degree of strength in terms of psychological feeling as well as physical feeling, and direction of goal orientation toward their future. The following data indicate the relation of the women's multiple roles to their perceived health and well-being.

Table 36

Self-Rated Health Status of the Respondents

Health Status	$\underline{N}$	%	Cumulated %
Excellent	3	4.1	4.1
Good	20	27.0	31.1
Fair	39	52.7	83.8
Don't know	2	2.7	86.5
Poor	8	10.8	97.3
Very poor	2	2.7	100.0
Total	74	100.0	

As shown in Table 36, about 31 percent of the Korean women rate themselves as in good or excellent health; about 53 percent of them rate themselves as in fair health. Even though the majority of the women report that they do not have any illnesses and are in good health, almost 50 percent of them report that they worry about future illness. The women's worry can be a response to their insecurity and unprotected working conditions.

Table 37

Cross Tabulation of Respondents' Working Hours Per Week, by Self-Rated Health Status of the Respondents

Working Hours	Health Status					Total (%)
	Excellent $\underline{N}$	Good $\underline{N}$	Fair $\underline{N}$	Poor $\underline{N}$	Very Poor $\underline{N}$	
31-40	2	2	6	2		12 (17.9)
41-50		5	11	1		17 (25.4)
51-60		7	15	3		25 (37.3)
61-70		3	4	1	1	9 (13.4)
71-80	1		1	1	1	4 (6.0)
Total	3	17	37	8	2	67
(%)	(4.5)	(25. 4)	(55.2)	(11.9)	(3.0)	(100.0)

Missing observations=7

When the Korean women's working hours exceed 40, only one woman indicates her present health as excellent. When the women's working hours exceed 60, 4.5 percent of the women rate their health as very good (see cross tabulation Table 37).

To identify the actual health conditions of the Korean women, the following questions were asked: Do you have any illnesses at the present time?; How many days have you felt sick during the last year?; How many days have you missed work during the last year?; and Do you worry a great deal about future illness? The majority of the Korean women (79.7%) do not have any illness at the present time. About 14 percent (10 respondents) of the women report that they have illnesses, including bad sight (1), chronic fatigue (1), obesity (1), indigestion (2), joint pain (2), leg ache (1), low blood pressure (1), shoulder ache (1), waist ache (2), etc. About one-third of the women have felt sick during the last year. They reported a mean of 9.3 days of feeling sick, ranging from one day to 90 days. Almost 40 percent of the women have not missed work during the last year. As a group they reported a mean of 6.4 days of work missed with a range from 3 days to 90 days. Regarding worry about future illness, half of the women indicate major worries about future illness, while another half of them report that they do not worry about it.

Table 38

Cross Tabulation of Respondents' Working Hours Per Week, by the Respondents' Worry About Future Illness

Working Hours	Worry About Future Illness		Total (%)
	Yes $\underline{N}$	No $\underline{N}$	$\underline{N}$
31-40	2	9	11 (16.7)
41-50	7	10	17 (25.8)
51-60	16	9	25 (37.9)
61-70	5	4	9 (13.6)
71-80	3	1	4 (6.1)
Total (%)	33	33	66(100.0)

Missing observations=8

The Korean women's worry about future illnesses shows a positive relationship with the number of hours they are working. When the women's working hours exceed 50 hours, more of them worry about future illnesses, as indicated in Table 38.

Table 39

Respondents' Self-Rated Degree of Strength in Psychological and Physical Aspects

Degree of Acceptance	Psychological		Physical	
	N	%	N	%
Definitely yes	15	20.3	9	12.2
Probably yes	35	47.3	24	32.4
Don't know	9	12.2	13	17.6
Probably not	12	16.2	24	32.4
Definitely not	3	4.1	4	5.4
Total	74	100.0	74	100.0

In self-rating the degree of their psychological and physical strength, almost 70 percent of the women report they are psychologically strong, while only about 45 percent report they are physically strong. In Table 36, more than 80 percent of the women report some degree of good health; however, Table 38 indicates that half of the women worry about their future illnesses. The following interviews represent the women's physical conditions in some detail. Mrs. A, 31 years old, does not have any illnesses at the present time, but she always feels tired. She lives with her husband, a salaried worker, her 5-year-old son, and a 3-year-old son. She has worked since 1989 when she came to the United States. She works about 10 hours a day. In addition, she spends about 3 to 5 hours on household work and caring for her children. Mrs. A said, "I feel sick every day, but I cannot take any rest. I think this is the life of immigrants. To spend time for leisure activity is a kind of dream to me. But someday . . . " A moment later Mrs. A continued "a religious belief always gives me a strong power. I strongly believe in my bright future."

Mrs. A's symptom, feeling sick, is also supported in other findings (see p. 94), indicating that about one-third of the Korean women feel sick. Another finding (see p. 62) indicates that about three-fourths of the women do not spend any time in leisure activities.

The sewing job requires a lot of physical energy as well as patience because of its long working hours. Mrs. R said, "It is a very hard job for women, in terms of the physical aspect. I think most of the working women in the apparel industry have overcome the obstacle with their psychological strength." Mrs. A said, "I am a strong woman psychologically, but I am not a strong woman physically. I am very tired every day, but I work hard every day for my children as well as for my family." Mrs A is a good example of the Korean women's psychological strength. As data in Table 39 show, almost 40 percent of the women indicate physical weakness, while about 20 percent of them report psychological weakness. It is obvious the Korean immigrant women contribute financially to their families despite their physical weaknesses. In the previous data reported in Table 10, more than 90 percent of the women indicate their financial contributions to their families.

Table 40

Direction of Respondents' Future Goal Orientation

Belief of Bright Future	$\underline{N}$	%	Cumulated %
Definitely yes	29	39.2	39.2
Probably yes	34	45.9	85.1
Don't know	10	13.5	98.6
Probably not	1	1.4	100.0
Definitely not	0	0.0	
Total	74	100.0	

The vast majority of the Korean women show their strong or moderately strong belief in a bright future in the United States, as indicated in Table 40. It reflects inexhaustible desire to achieve their goals of successful life in this country.

Table 41

Cross Tabulation of Direction of Respondents' Future Goal Orientation, by the Respondents' Year of Arriving in the U.S.

Belief of Bright Future	Year of Arriving in the U.S.			Total (%)
	1974-79	1980-85	1986-90	
	N	N	N	
Definitely yes	10	7	12	29 (40.8)
Probably yes	7	13	14	34 (47.9)
Don't know		1	6	7 (9.9)
Probably not			1	1 (1.4)
Total (%)	17(23.9)	21(29.6)	33(46.5)	71 (100.0)

Missing observations= 3

Regardless of the length of residence of the Korean women in the United States, almost 90 percent of those responding to the question report that they believe they have a bright future in the United States. About 10 percent of them gave no response to the question, and only one woman reported that she probably will not have a bright future (see cross tabulation Table 41).

In summary, in terms of self-rated health, the majority of the women report that they do not have any illness at present; however, about one-third of them have felt sick during the last year; and almost 50 percent of them worry about future illnesses. Almost 70 percent of the women report they are psychologically strong, while only about 45 percent report themselves to be physically strong. Regardless of the length of residence in the United States, almost 90 percent of the women indicate their belief in a bright future in the United States. Thus they have high expectations of life in the United States. The women's multiple roles seem to be positively related to psychological strength and negatively related to physical health.

Summary

Through the analysis of these research findings, familial, work, and social roles and the perceived health and well-being of some Korean women were described. The familial role was identified as the most important role among the women, followed by the social role and then the work role. The women's perceived health was reported as good; however, the women also voiced their worry about future illnesses and about feeling sick. The following chapter will apply a hermeneutical analysis to these data.

Chapter 5

Korean Married Immigrant Women Working In The Dallas Apparel Industry: A Hermeneutic Approach

Linge (1977, xii) maintains that the application of hermeneutics occurs in all situations in which we encounter meanings not immediately understandable. Therefore, hermeneutics has a role as a bridge between "the familiar world" we understand and "the strange meaning" we strive to understand. The tasks of hermeneutics are, on the one hand, to ascertain exact meaning-content of a word, sentence, and text and, on the other hand, to discover the instructions contained in the symbolic forms (Bleicher 1980, 11). The purpose of this section is to interpret the experiences of Korean immigrant women working in the Dallas apparel industry from the hermeneutical approach. In doing so, the following four steps of Ricoeur's hermeneutics are applied: (1) explanation of the motives of the actors; (2) analysis of the text's structure; (3) appropriation; and (4) critical reflection. For this study, the texts used were the results of in-depth interviews with Korean women working in the Dallas apparel industry, the notes taken during the in-depth interviews, field notes from the workplace, and the responses to questionnaire as reported in Chapter IV.

Explanation of the Motives of the Actors

The first step of Ricoeur's theory of textual understanding is to connect the relations between explanation and understanding (Ricoeur 1981, 149-151). Explanation is applied to such manifestations, to such testimonies, to such monuments, of which understanding provides the basis in the paired understanding-explanation. From the interplay of explanation and understanding, the initial image can be tested, corrected, and deepened by the text (Klemm 1983, 91). Therefore, Ricoeur (1978c, 165) insists that the explanatory method and the method of understanding are not two separate approaches.

> Understanding is rather the non-methodic moment which, in the sciences of interpretation, comes together with the methodic moment of explanation. Understanding precedes, accompanies, closes, and thus envelops explanation.

In return, explanation develops understanding analytically.

In order to find out what motivate the Korean women in this study to work in the United States, it is necessary to review occupational conditions for married women in Korea, to identify the major support networks of Korean working women in the United States, and to analyze the function that garment jobs play in the Korean immigrant families.

The Korean women who are the focus of this study came to the United States from Korea during the period from 1974 to 1990. Mrs. R's case well reflects the women's, especially the married women's, employment conditions in Korea. Mrs. R, 38 years old, who has been working in the apparel industry for 10 years, lives with her husband, a 12-year-old daughter, and a 16-year-old son. Before she was married in Korea, she worked as a secretary in a large company. When she married, she had to leave the company, even though this was not her choice. Most Korean companies did not hire married women in the early 1970s. Under these social conditions, Korean working women could not have marriage and a career at the same time. Therefore, Mrs. R is very happy that she can work in the United States, even though her Korean high-school education overqualifies her for work in the apparel industry. One of the reasons for Mrs. R's willingness to work in the apparel industry is her poor command of the English language. Mrs.

R's case is typical of the women who have minimal knowledge of English. Most of the women also have minor children. However, after coming to the United States, the women did not want to stay at home; rather, they wanted to participate in the labor force to improve their families' living conditions.

Major social support networks of the Korean women were identified as relatives, Korean neighbors, and friends. Through the supportive relationships, the women could get valuable information such as job resources and child care. Even though the women obtained some help from the social support network, the support network was very limited within the Korean community in the Dallas area. The primary barrier to entrance into the main society in the United States seemed to be their lack of skills in the English language. The women's language handicap also seemed related to their lack of contacts in the United States. The women showed a strong desire to educate their children to improve their children's occupational opportunities in the United States. They believe their children's academic success will guarantee a bright future in the United States. They also believe that living conditions for their children's generation will be better than that for their parents' generations, particularly in terms of professional careers. The following statement by Mrs. R represents the Korean women's wish for their children's success: "My children (a 16-year-old boy and a 12-year-old girl) have been educated in the United States. . . . They will get a good job. . . . The life of my children's generation should be different from their parents' generation, I believe." The Korean women's strong desire to educate their children reflects a parental spirit of self-sacrifice and a pioneering effort for their children.

To achieve their successful life in the United States, the women began to work in the apparel industry. The women's work in the apparel industry helped the Korean immigrant family not only in the beginning stage, but also in the later, more settled stage. The women's strong desire to achieve their financial success supported them and gave them strength to endure hardships in the apparel industry.

Mrs. L's case shows how a sewing job supported the Korean immigrant family financially in the beginning stage. Mrs. L is 35 years old, lives with her husband, a 10-year-old and a 2-year-old daughter in a nice house in a middle-class neighborhood. She has worked in the apparel industry since 1985 when she came to the United States and started in a sewing job. Mrs. L encouraged her husband to acquire some technical skills. He decided to take a course in a technical school for 6 months. Mrs. L was the breadwinner while Mr. L was in training. Mr. L is now working as a welder and earning about $1,000 weekly. Mrs. L is still working as a home sewer. Since she does not have any financial pressure, she enjoys working and saves most of her earnings. Mrs. L mentioned her husband's strong desire to secure an education for their children. According to Mrs. L, her husband feels something lacking about the fact that they do not have a baby boy. However, Mr. L and Mrs. L have great concerns about their children's education. Their 10-year-old daughter Q takes lessons in music, TaeKwonDo, and drawing. In addition, Q has taught by a private tutor at home. It reflects her parents' expectations for their daughter. One of the happiest moments common to all the Korean parents is when their children make good grades.

Three strong motivational forces show up in the Korean women's work histories. First of all, their motive to work explains the women's strong intention to be independent and contribute financially for the sake of their families. Their native country of Korea provided few job opportunities for women, especially for married women. For the women, the possibility that they could get a job was a factor which attracted them to the United States. The women did not hesitate to work, even in an area which is not considered appropriate given their educational levels. The women's economic participation has opened up new roles, changing their traditional women's roles. In a traditional Korean family, the man dominates in public affairs, while the woman takes full responsibility in the family (Kim 1976, 49). The woman is not expected to participate in the labor force. Secondly, the women's will to work reflects their determination to contribute to their families' financial stability. The women show independence, strong activity, and spontaneity in improving their families' financial conditions. The women chose not to be bystanders; they did not persist in only a familial role. Finally, the strong work motivation reflects the Korean women's challenge and courage in a new world where they believe their dreams will come true in the near future.

Analysis of the Text's Structure

The text provides the opportunity for understanding, and it provides the possibility of broadening one's horizon in unexpected directions.

Above all, the text gives rise to a chain of interpretations (Klemm 1983, 82). Interpretation involves a pre-hermeneutical meaning and an analysis of objective sense. Analysis can confirm and highlight some of the pre-hermeneutical meaning of texts. According to Klemm (1983, p. 95), structural analysis is an essential stage between "naive comprehension and a sophisticated one." When one reads a simple-meaning text, the sense of the text points to a perceivable referent against the perceptual world. Then in the next step, the literary text requires interpretative effort. The literary text presents the figurative and suggestive power of language in its capacity to describe something in the world. In Ricoeur's (1981, 133) discussion of the structural analysis of language, he acknowledged the necessity of considering language as an event in addition to language as a system of signs. As an event, language is usually considered as speech or discourse and is distinguished from language as a system by a number of traits: it is realized temporarily; it is self-referential; it is about something, refers to a world outside itself; and it is aimed at an addressee (Bleicher 1980, 229).

The text reveals how the women were motivated to take garment jobs. As shown in the previous stage, the women grew up in a society in which women's work opportunities were very limited. Therefore, it is natural that the women are interested in the information provided by their relatives, neighbors, and friends about the garment industry. Working opportunity itself is very attractive to the women who had been deprived of work opportunities in Korea. This condition encouraged the women to start on the lowest rung of occupation without hesitation.

Some of the women perceive downward mobility in their social class in the United States as opposed to their social class in Korea. However, the women are not negative about their past life in Korea; rather, they show positive, future-oriented attitudes toward living in the United States. Mrs. P's case reflects the women's future-oriented attitude. Mrs. P, 38 years old, has been working in the apparel industry for 5 years. She works more than 10 hours every day to fulfill her dream of being a self-employed owner of an alteration shop. Mrs. K, who has had 2 years working experiences in the garment industry, describes the sewing job as "the very first step for immigrants." Now she has a small sandwich shop business. The women see advantages and disadvantages to working in the apparel industry. The great advantage is flexibility of working hours, allowing the women to handle their familial roles such as doing household work and taking care of children. However, in addition to the advantages, some disadvantages are also identified by the women.

Because of the subordinate relationship of subcontractors to a main company and competition among the subcontractors, the garment business seems unstable at the present time. Mr. B, who is the owner of an apparel company, represents the apparel job as "legal slavery." He said:

> I am an owner in this company, but I do not think I am an owner here. If the main company does not provide previously cut garments, there is no way to remain in this business.

As a result of instability in the garment business, the Korean working women face some difficulty; income, especially, is not secure. There are peak seasons and off seasons in the industry. The pay per garment is too low and remains constant. These facts of life in the garment industry push the women to work extremely long hours. During the off season, some of the women have to find other garment companies to work for. The insecure relationships between the employees and the employers impede development in the apparel industry.

The apparel industry does not provide good working conditions or benefits for employees. Typical working conditions in the apparel industry are crowded, cramped, and excessively noisy. Dust and threads from fabrics make the working conditions even worse. Ventilation is poor. There are no rest areas, or extra benefits for overtime work. There is a lot of physical stress coming from long working hours as well as psychological stress from the work which demands meeting a deadline. Unfortunately, the apparel industry does not offer health insurance to employees. Although the majority of the women rate themselves as being in good health, some of them worry about future illness and feeling sick. Mrs. A, 31 years old, described her physical condition as follows: "I feel sick every day, but I cannot take any rest. I think this is the life of immigrants." Mrs. A works about 10 hours a day as a sewer. "I am a strong woman psychologically, but I am not a strong woman physically," she said, "I am very tired every day, but I work hard every day for my children as well as for my family."

Even with the conditions of the apparel industry, with inadequate benefits to employees, half of the women voiced satisfaction with their working conditions, suggesting the women's acceptance of their low status. The women are so grateful to their employers, who provide them a job, that they feel they cannot complain. Such acceptance reflects the women's patience and goal-oriented attitude in adapting to their roles in the apparel industry. The women's attitude about their work indicates their lack of resistance in challenging their present condition. Under the patriarchal structure in Korea, women did not have an opportunity to improve their social skills. Since the women's activities in Korea were very limited, especially in the work area, their present perspectives come from their socialization to traditional women's roles. According to Koh Hesung (1983, 159), many Korean men and women still have the idea that the goal of equality is a Western ideal rather than a Korean ideal. Therefore, both the intellectuals and the general public believe that there are no harmful effects from the present inequality. The Korean working women did not display much regard for their own work roles. Therefore, it is natural that they are ignored in terms of health or other benefits. As Mrs. L's case shows, she encouraged her husband to get a better job and shows a strong desire to educate her child; however, she does not show any interest in development for herself. She seems relatively happy.

Most Korean women would feel honored and rewarded as wives and mothers for their contribution when their husbands and sons succeed in public life. This tradition derives from the historical fact that Korean women were anonymous in social life because they did not have their own names in earlier times. Even today, a woman is not identified by her own name in casual talk but in connection with her parents, husband, and children. A woman is referred to as the daughter of her parents before marriage, as the wife of her husband after marriage, and as the mother of her children after having children. Even today many Korean married women live in a faceless and anonymous world like Mrs. L. Some of the women interviewed in this study suggested that they are not happy with the present inequality. Mrs. R said that "it is a physically hard job for women." Almost half of the women indicated that their living conditions in Korea were better than in the United States.

The apparel industry includes the following figurative meanings. First of all, like the past, the apparel industry is a place which provides the motive for some immigrants' struggle for financial success through the accumulation of capital. Second, the apparel industry is a place that takes advantage of women's status as married with minor children and uses immigrants who lack skill in the English language. Third, the apparel industry is a place in which the main company deals with subcontractors through excessive competition among the subcontractors. Finally, the apparel industry is a place which exploits immigrant women's cheap labors in poor working conditions and patriarchal structure.

Appropriation

Klemm (1983, 140-144) maintains that at the stage of appropriation, the meaning of the text is defined in familiarity. In the beginning, the reader tries to follow the sense of the referent as an experience within an interpreted world. When the reader recognizes the text as a mode of being "my own," he or she appropriates the referent. In appropriation, an imagined possibility happens in actual fact. The shift from understanding the other to understanding the world of his or her work indicates a shift in the "hermeneutical circle." Ricoeur (1978b, 144) indicates that the "hermeneutical circle" cannot obtain simply from a scientific, objective procedure; rather it involves the reader's precomprehension of his or her world. According to Ricoeur (1978b, 145-146), the circle of understanding occurs "between my mode of being--beyond the knowledge which I may have of it--and the way of being disclosed by the text as the work's world."

The first two stages show how the women get into the garment industry and what experiences the inexperienced women had in the workplace. The women's experiences in the garment industry tell how the Korean subcontractors are intertwined with their contractors and as a result they are exploited as sources of cheap labor.

In spite of the women's lack of a professional attitude toward their work roles, their long working hours reflect their strong desire to work, even without a well developed identity as workers. This outcome is no doubt the result of a socialization process which is deeply rooted in the patriarchal structure. The women's attitudes toward their roles seem to be a result of their cultural background. Usually, the Korean woman's work is expected to be fulfilled within the household, while the man's work is expected to be done outside the household. Therefore, in the Korean language, the house wife is called "inside master," *ahn chuin*, while the house head is called "outside master," *pakkat chuin* (Sorensen 1983, 70).

The social status of Korean women has been historically low. During the Yi dynasty (1392-1910), women's social activities were restricted to those for which they could get permission from either their husbands or the head of their families. The rulers of the Yi dynasty believed that the disorder in the previous Koryo dynasty was partly due to women's frequent involvement in social activities. Through the Yi dynasty, even women's outdoor games were prohibited in the name of public order, except for the early period (Kim 1976, 83-85). Korean women's position in the family during the Yi dynasty also is revealed in the following rules:

(1) Only those in the paternal line of relatives were regarded as relatives.

(2) Social class and rights were transmitted only from fathers to sons.

(3) The sole authority in the family rested with the father who held control over the children.

(4) Marriages were allowed only with those outside the blood clan.

(5) First-born males held the right to lineal succession (Kim 1976, 89).

Steinberg (1989, 76-77) points out that today, although there are constitutional guarantees of the rights of women, Korean women are still subjected to unfair treatment by laws. In addition, Koreans viewed negatively the influence of women, even informal influence. Strong and outspoken Korean women's activities were often criticized as *ch'ima param* ("the wind of the skirts").

The Korean women in this study were raised in a patriarchal society, and their conception of gender roles is internalized from that society. The women accept the man's role as breadwinner and the woman's role as housekeeper. In addition, the women accept domestic labor and women's subordinate position to men as a woman's natural role. On the other hand, the women in this study wanted to be secure financially. Also, they tried to cooperate with their husbands to achieve their families' financial security. Even though the women showed inconsistency regarding gender roles, their willingness to work is a great challenge to the traditional perspective. The women's attitudinal change, to work not only for their families but also for themselves, could be a motivational factor regarding their work roles. Work for some women is a first step, but further steps will determine the women's future status. Also, the Korean women's strong capacity for living, their psychological strength, their patience, and spirit of sacrifice should be considered as virtue.

Critical Reflection

Finally, the hermeneutics of texts includes a reader's subjectivity in interpretations. The world of the text takes the place of the author's subjectivity. And, at the same time, the author's subjectivity is displaced by the reader's subjectivity (Ricoeur 1986, 331-332). Now we live in a society which expects that women have more than the familial roles, but that society is still structured in a traditional way. When women perform more than their family role, they add many burdens. Women's working roles are often ignored in terms of their importance. According to Mies (1986, 37-38), the literal meaning of "patriarchy" is the rule of fathers. However, today, patriarchy includes the rule of husbands, of male bosses, and of ruling men in most societal institutions such as politics and economics. Mies states that in a historical sense, the concept of patriarchy refers to women's exploitation and oppression. Today, patriarchal systems are almost universal, although the systems were developed at a particular time, by particular people in particular geographical areas. Now the systems link to capitalism. Mies believes that patriarchal man-woman relations are necessary to maintain a capitalistic system. Mies (1986, 38) maintains that patriarchy constitutes "the mostly invisible underground of the visible capitalist system." Therefore, Mies points out, women's problems cannot be explained simply by mentioning the old form of patriarchal structure.

Within a patriarchal system, women's wishes to be equal to men cannot be achieved, unless they want to be like those patriarchal men. Therefore, as Mies (1986, 37) points out, women could "build up a non-hierarchical, non-centralized society" to be equal to men in a true sense of equality not in a power struggle.

The texts show the women's courage in supporting themselves in adverse circumstances such as bad working conditions, physical weaknesses, and downward social mobility. These women have been sacrificed, to some degree, under a patriarchal society which demands patience, silence, and concession as women's virtues; yet the indomitable wills and future-oriented attitudes of the women must be recognized as virtues or, at the very least, they must be acknowledged.

This research represents an example of the patriarchal society which regards women's labor-force participation as a temporary or a secondary role, while women's traditional household work still exists as a primary role. Under the patriarchal structure, women suffer double burdens from their economic participation with low wages and their traditional women's roles. Bernard (1987, 19) maintains that almost everywhere women spend a considerable amount of their life time in child-bearing and child-rearing activities; however, they also do work-related activities which take up a considerable amount of time. One aspect of a patriarchal society is to use women's labor at society's convenience. In a Korean family, the wife has responsibility for managing the family economy. It seems that the wife has a powerful influence within the family; however, if the husband's earnings are not enough to support the family, the wife has to make up for the shortage as is the case of the women in this study. Usually, when the husband's earnings are high, the husband has the power to make final decisions for managing family incomes. The wife has a responsibility to manage the family budget, such as grocery shopping, the purchase of clothes for family members, expenses for children's education, and other household items for her family. The husband, on the other hand, has the power to manage the family economy, in such things as purchasing a house or car, investing in real estate or stock, and other higher-priced items.

These Korean women work apparently not because of feminism or attitudinal change, but rather as a way of supporting their families in a new cultural setting and of producing necessary income to improve the futures of their children. In the family, as Mrs. P's case shows, the conception of sex roles is still controlled by the patriarchal structure. Mrs. P, 38 years old, has an 11-year-old son and a 13-year-old daughter. She is a home seamstress. She works 60 hours per week. She spends 3 to 4 hours a day in household work. Her family members participate in household work often, except the son. Mrs. P's daughter's assigned job is the laundry; however, Mrs. P does not expect any help from her son. She does not even want to let her son participate in household work because "he is a boy." Mrs. P is one example of how sex-role expectations differ for daughters and sons. Many Korean families still have the same sex-role conception as Mrs. P. A notion of favoring a son to a daughter also shows in educational attaintment by sex. According to the 1990 census, Korean men had higher rates of 4-year college graduates (46.9%) than Korean women (25.9%). Mrs. R, 38 years old, stated her opinion about married women's careers as follows:

> I believe the husband's occupation is more important than the wife's occupation. If a married couple faces a situation, in which they cannot hold their jobs together, then, wife should give up her job. I know it is not fair, but it is our reality. This is a way to keep the family peaceful.

Even in the family, women are in a secondary position. The family is the first place where children learn and internalize gender roles. Especially, the mother's role in the early socialization process exerts an important influence on the children. Therefore, a change of woman's consciousness regarding gender-role equality could become a driving force to stimulate reexamining gender stereotypes. Women could raise their voices for their equal rights. Women could have a work role for self-development. Women could develop their self-esteem in social activities. Women could be united to improve their status. Women could have a firm identity about themselves and be proud of themselves. Without women's awareness that they have been given unfair status in the name of patriarchal structure, they will be permanent shadows of men. Women could apply social pressure by using traditional women's traits. Korean women who have lived in the shadow could no longer be characterized as faceless, voiceless, and powerless.

In summary, throughout the hermeneutic analysis, the impact of the patriarchy is visible in the family as well as in the workplace. The following chapter will include a general summary and conclusions of the study.

Chapter 6

SUMMARY AND CONCLUSIONS OF THE STUDY

The purpose of this study was to describe the familial, work, and social roles and the perceived health and well-being of Korean immigrant women working in the Dallas apparel industry. A review of the literature includes some discussion of the following: 1) patterns of Korean immigration to the United States; 2) Korean immigrant women in the United States; 3) married women's roles within the family; 4) patriarchy and the female labor market; 5) women in the apparel industry; and 6) minority women's experiences in the United States. The research questions were addressed under the following five specific categories: 1) demographic characteristics; 2) familial roles; 3) work roles; 4) social roles; and 5) perceived health and well-being.

A multi-method approach was used to answer the research questions. The methodology of the present research included library research, survey research, and field research. For the survey research, a questionnaire and in-depth interviews were administered. For the field research, complete observation was conducted. The questionnaire was administered to a non-random sample of 74 Korean immigrant women who worked for a Korean-owned apparel company. The data collection process took approximately 6 months, from March to August of 1991. A snowball technique was used to select the respondents who were willing to participate in this study. The respondents were contacted individually in their homes, workplaces, or churches. In-depth interviews were conducted with 13 informants. The in-depth interviews were conducted one time each, taking from a half hour to 2 hours. Each was recorded in notes or on audiotape. In addition, complete observations from the workplace and home setting were conducted, and these data were collected as systematic field notes.

The method of data analysis in this study included descriptive and hermeneutic approaches. The data from the questionnaire were analyzed using quantitative procedures available through SPSSx computer programs. Descriptive statistics, including frequency tables, and cross tabulation charts were used. Qualitative procedures were used to analyze categories which emerged from the data themselves. Field notes from the complete observation were analyzed in terms of hermeneutical theory. In-depth interviews were conducted with the president of the Korean Texas Garment Contractor's Association, with employers, managers, ex-employees, and sewing employees in garment companies. These interviews were used to present the garment companies' business and work environment.

Demographic Characteristics of Sample Korean Working Women in the Apparel Industry in Dallas, Texas, Area

The majority of the women in this study (85%) are between 30 and 49 years of age. The median age is 38 years, and the mean age is 38.3 years. The majority of the women are married. More than half of the women (52.7%) indicate a nuclear family type of living with their husbands and/or their children. The average number of children is 1.9. About 44 percent of the women have minor children under 12 years old. All of the women came to the United States between 1974 and 1990. Almost half of the women came to the United States between 1986 and 1990. The length of time the women have been in the United States seems to correlate with the type of residence. The women who have lived in the United States for more than 5 years are more likely to have their own homes, while those who have lived in the United States for less than 5 years are more likely to live in rented houses.

All of the women had at least some education in Korea. The majority of the women (69.4%) report that they "completed high school" in Korea. More than 95 percent of the women had no education at all in the United States. The majority have difficulty with the English language, no doubt related to their lack of contacts in the United States. Concerning the present occupation of the women's husbands, more blue-collar jobs (68%) than white-collar jobs (32%) are reported. In this study, all of the women are sewers. Their average length of working experience is 5.8 years in the apparel company and 2.9 years in the present company. The average monthly income is $1,380 for the women, $3,096 for the women and their spouses.

Familial Roles

More than 50 percent of the women willingness to give up their jobs immediately when their households no longer need their financial contributions. About 35 percent of the women desire to continue to work in the apparel industry regardless of need. The vast majority of the Korean women do not manage their income independently; rather they put their earnings together with their spouses' as family income. The Korean women's economic participation seems to be very important to their families, with more than 90 percent reporting that they contribute to their families' financial well-being. The vast majority (91.8%) of the women say their family members participate in housework. More than 90 percent of the Korean women spend fewer than 6 hours per day doing housework. The median hours spent doing housework are 4 hours per day and mean hours are 3.9. Compared with McAllister's study (1990) in Australia, the Korean working women spend fewer hours in household labor than Australian working women.

The Korean women themselves, their husbands, and the children's grandparents are the major sources of child care. About 34 percent of the women show some degree of satisfaction with the time they spend with their children, while about 40 percent of them report some degree of dissatisfaction with this aspect of their family life. This study supports the work of Fox et al. (1984) showing that many employed people feel uncertain about the care of their children. The vast majority of the married women (95%) spend less than 5 hours a day taking care of their children. In-depth interviews with three Korean married working women in the garment industry were used to represent the strategy of child care, housework participation, and feeling about the time spent with children.

Only a quarter of the Korean women have some leisure activities. Because of the busy schedule of the working women, their leisure activities and kinship obligations seem to be limited and individualistic. Almost 60 percent of the women are very or somewhat satisfied with their familial roles, while almost 25 percent are somewhat dissatisfied with their roles within the family. Regardless of the length of working hours of the Korean women, about 70 percent of them think women should have a subordinate position to their husbands in the family.

Work Roles

The Korean women learned how to sew from a variety of sources: a neighbor, a friend, a relative, another sewing company, from self-practice, or from an apparel institution in Korea. Salary is indicated as the most important factor when the Korean working women choose a company. Other factors are listed as follows: working conditions, position, employer, and location. More than 80 percent of the women work more than 40 hours per week. The mean working hours are 53.7 hours per week. Only about 40 percent of the women indicate that their positions are very or moderately important in the present company. About 68 percent of the women have a positive feeling toward working women in general. Concerning their present working conditions and their present company, a little more than half of the women show some degree of satisfaction. The majority of the women (75.7%) have a good relationship with their employers in general. None of them has a definitely bad relationship with their employers.

The majority of the women (73%) do not have medical insurance. In fact, none of the apparel industries in this study have sick-leave benefits. Concerning the women's desires to stay in the apparel industry, 45 percent of them wish to leave the apparel industry immediately, and about 36 percent of them want to stay in the apparel industry as long as they remain physically able to work. In general, the apparel industry is perceived as providing equal opportunity regardless of sex. None of the women believes that males get better positions than females in the present company. Concerning the women's satisfaction with their present incomes, given their educational level, more than half of them believe their incomes are not reasonable in some respects. More than half of the Korean women have some degree of satisfaction in the apparel industry; however, about 90 percent of them do not prefer the apparel industry as their children's future careers. The great advantage of working in the apparel industry is flexibility of working hours. In addition to this advantage, three major disadvantages were identified by the women: the low pay for garments, long working hours, and bad ventilation.

In-depth interviews with four Korean working women and one employer in the apparel industry were used to show how the women enter the apparel industry, how their working in the apparel industry supports their family, why they chose the apparel job, the advantages and/or disadvantages of working in the apparel industry, and why the women do not prefer the apparel industry as their children's future work area. In addition, field notes helped to describe the apparel business, the working conditions of two companies and the conditions in the homes of two home sewers. Working conditions in most of the apparel companies are poor, obviously crowded, cramped, and excessively noisy. Even though working conditions in home settings are better than in the company buildings, there still remains the problem of dust from the garments.

Social Roles

The majority of the women (59.4%) perceive themselves as middle class. By coming to the United States, the women hoped to achieve a better education for their children and financial stability for their families. Almost 50 percent of the women believe that their living conditions in Korea were better than in the United States. Despite the women's long working hours (53.7 mean hours per week), more than 80 percent of them accept a woman's natural role as that of domestic laborer. Almost 60 percent of the women indicate their acceptance of the man's role as breadwinner and of the woman's role as housekeeper and child rearer. The vast majority of the women (87.7%) feel positively about women working in general. About 85 percent of the women believe they should receive wages equal to those given men in the same job capacity.

Regarding women's present status in the family, as well as in our society, more than half of the women have positive feelings. The women perceive their roles as being most important in the family

(96%), followed by other roles, in society (51%), and, last, in the workplace (40%). Regarding the women's degree of contribution to the Korean-American Community, about 37 percent of them do contribute, while about 40 percent of them do not contribute to the Korean-American Community. Only 17.6 percent of the women have successfully achieved their goals in the United States; however, about 85 percent of them believe in a bright future in the United States. One of the happiest moments common to all the Korean parents is when their children make good grades.

Perceived Health and Well-Being

In terms of self-rated health, about 84 percent of the Korean women rate their health as good or fair. The majority of them (79.7%) do not have any illnesses at the present time. However, almost 50 percent of them worry about future illness. The women's self-rated degree of psychological and physical strength shows a perception of physical weakness (37.8%) over psychological weakness (20.3%). Regardless of the length of residence in the United States, almost 90 percent of the women believe they have a bright future in the United States.

Conclusion

Korean women were very restricted by the traditional culture and structure of Korean society. Usually women were portrayed as subordinate and dependent beings, rather than as creative, independent beings. For instance until 1910, the end of the Yi Dynasty, wives could be divorced by husbands on any one of seven grounds: (1) disobeying the husband's parents, (2) failing to have children, (3) acquiring a loathsome disease, (4) committing adultery, (5) displaying jealousy, (6) being overly talkative, and (7) stealing. There were no reasons husbands could be divorced by wives. The example shows the subordination of traditional Korean women. Although these rules do not apply to the present Korean woman, the majority are still isolated and oppressed by their family roles and by society. In most cases, a Korean married woman's status is judged by her husband's position.

In Korean society, women's roles are still largely restricted within the family while men's economic roles are considered superior to women's roles. As a result, the domestic labors of women are regarded as a woman's natural role and seen as inferior to men's roles. This research found the familial role to be the most important role among the Korean garment workers. However, the economic conditions in the United States make it necessary for immigrant women to work. Especially among the immigrant family, women's economic participation is a great contribution to the adaptation to a new society. Accordingly, women are required to play multi-roles by engaging in economic activities, voluntarily or involuntarily. Thus the present patriarchal structure, focusing on traditional gender roles, leads to confusion and ambivalence. For example, in this study, a majority of the Korean immigrant working women indicate that women should receive wages equal to those of men in the same job capacity. However, the women indicate their acceptance of the man's role as breadwinner and the woman's role as housekeeper and mother. In addition, the women report that women should have a subordinate position to their husbands in the family. Ironically, the women want to be treated equally regardless of their gender in the workplace; however, the women also show their dependency on their husbands in the family. Such contradictory attitudes seem to be related to the socialization process which is deeply rooted in the patriarchal structure of Korea.

This research showed labor-market segmentation of immigrants with low wages in a labor-intensive enterprise. In this study, more than 80 percent of the Korean women work more than 40 hours per week; however, only about 40 percent of them indicate the importance of their positions in the present company. The women's alienation from the work in which they participate can be explained by Marx's concept of the alienation from labor. Clearly the working women do not identify themselves primarily as working women. Rather, as working women, they still accept the importance of traditional gender roles. This finding suggests a confusion or ambiguity of roles resulting from demands of the Korean patriarchal structure to which they were socialized and the reality demands of everyday life in the United States. Figure 2 shows the process of the formation of the Korean women's role in the United States. The figure presents how patriarchal structure and capitalism lead to the women's new familial roles and how the women disclose two contradictory gender roles in the family and the workplace. The figure 2 also reveals the hierarchical structure of the garment industry which

Figure 2

The Process of the Korean Women's Role Formation

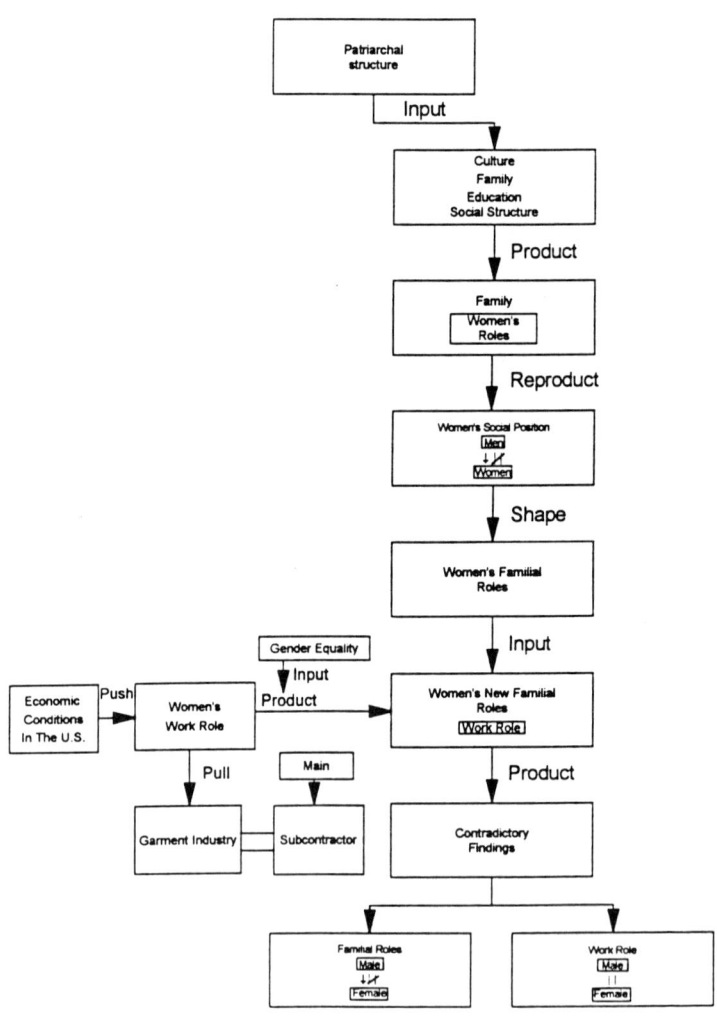

depends on the women as sources of low labor. The impact of the concept of gender equality in the workplace creates the women's new perspective about their roles, but produces contradictory findings. Through this research, there is little sense of feminist tendencies in the women. The women did not state that they wish for equality with their spouses or bosses, except in the area of pay.

In "Women's History in Public: 'Picture Brides' of Hawaii," Chai (1988) used the feminist approach of viewing Korean and Japanese women as active political strategists and creators of a women-centered women's culture and approached women as "whole human beings." Chai and her colleagues interviewed Korean and Japanese picture brides, collected photographs of these women, and provided analytical concepts to write the script for an audio tape to go with a slide show. The picture brides of 1910 challenged stereotypes and generalizations about gender roles in Asian immigrant communities (Chai 1988, 56). The ideal of Korean women's gentle submission was surpassed by the women's activities as creative independent beings. Most of the Korean picture brides went against their parents' wishes in going to Hawaii. From the Korean brides' perspective, the picture marriage fulfilled for them a dream of living abroad and freedom from the groom's family. The picture brides encouraged their husbands to change their occupations, and many of the sugar plantation workers moved to urban areas, particularly to Honolulu (Choy 1979, 101). On the other hand, many of the picture brides bought properties and started businesses without the consent of their husbands or the help of their children.

Among the picture brides, female solidarity through female friendship, women's groups, strong Christian faith, and memories of their mothers' and grandmothers' strengths were common. Many of the women were major financial providers for their families and were able to visit Korea because they had joined the women's *Key* (private financial association) group to finance their trips, and had control over their own income (Chai 1988, 56). Within the family, the picture brides did well in their roles and in their private worlds. The picture brides lived during a period when the concept of feministic perspective did not exist, about 80 years ago.

Compared with the story of the picture brides in the 1910s, the Korean women in the apparel industry in 1990s do not show any substantial feministic inclinations in the family or in the workplace. The Korean women in the apparel industry are more educated than the picture brides. However, apparently education alone does not change women's conception of sex roles. These findings suggest that patriarchal structures are deeply rooted in Korean society, even in higher education. In the *Female World from a Global Perspective*, Bernard (1987, 27) states that "The whole educational system, which separates girls and boys at the earliest age, is designed to make girls aware of what women should be." As she points out, sex-role segregation is visible not only in school but also in the family.

Without a new perspective regarding gender roles focused on equality, women's confusion concerning their roles will remain as a residual of the patriarchal structure. This confusion is but a thread in the patriarchal cloth of society. If women are willing to challenge their former traditions and norms, the thread can weave innovative cloth. However, such change is possible only with women's willingness to become pioneers in changing women's roles.

Following are some suggestions for improving the working conditions of the Korean immigrant women in the Dallas garment industry. Working hours are extremely long. Regulations of overtime, safe ventilation, and resting areas are essential. Second, child-care centers need to be supplied for working mothers with minor children. Since the women do not want to use a nursery for child care, a child-care center should be especially designed for the Korean children. Third, preventive health care should be provided for the women workers because this study shows that half of the women worry about future illness. Preventive care must include regular check-ups and health insurance.

Finally, the women need service programs, such as English language classes, family therapy, and educational courses for working women. To improve the conditions for the women, the Korean community in Dallas, as well as the apparel industry employers, must be willing to cooperate. Perhaps, the diminished importance of gender roles for women created by the old patriarchal structure helped to motivate a feminist challenge for the Korean women as they begin to seek equality with men both financially and socially.

APPENDIX

Dear Respondents!

I am a female graduate student in the department of Sociology and Social Work at Texas Woman's University . I am conducting a survey of female Korean immigrants' conditions in the apparel industry and their roles in the United States. The study is my dissertation and is approved by TWU.

Your responses to this study will be used for this study only, and it will be collected anonymously for your privacy. If you participate willingly and answer frankly, this study will be valuable basic material for understanding female Korean immigrants especially those who are working in the apparel industry. Your participation is strongly urged. Thank You!

Researcher: Shin Ja Um

Direction: Check or circle one answer to each question, unless otherwise specified, or answer in the space provided.

Demographic Characteristics

1. Marital Status: Single Married Divorced Widowed Other
   (Circle One)

2. If you have children, how many do you have?
   (List age and sex)

3. If you are married, what is your husband's present occupation?

4. Who works in your household besides you?

5. How long have you worked in the apparel industry?

6. How long have you worked for the present company?

7. What kind of skill(s) do you have?

8. Present age:

9. The highest educational level achieved in Korea:

10. The highest educational level achieved in the United States:

11. How is your spoken English?
    - (1) Fluent
    - (2) Good
    - (3) Fair
    - (4) Poor
    - (5) Not at all

12. How is your reading of English?
    - (1) Fluent
    - (2) Good
    - (3) Fair
    - (4) Poor
    - (5) Not at all

13. How is your written English?
    - (1) Fluent
    - (2) Good
    - (3) Fair
    - (4) Poor
    - (5) Not at all

14. Date of arrival in the United States:

15. Date of arrival in the Dallas area:

16. Your last occupation in Korea:
    (Include husband's occupation, if you are married)

17. Current income in the United States:
    - (1) How often are you paid?
    - (2) What is your average pay check?
    - (3) Are you paid by the hour or piece?

18. Current family income in the United States:
    - (1) How often are your family members paid?
    - (2) What is the amount of your family members' average pay checks?

19. Type of residence: own home, rent home, apartment, other
    (Circle One)

20. With whom do you live now?
    - (1) Alone
    - (2) Husband
    - (3) Children
    - (4) Mother
    - (5) Father
    - (6) Mother-in-law
    - (7) Father-in-law
    - (8) Others (Please describe)

Familial Roles

21. How much of your salary do you contribute to your family's
    (1) Clothes? _____
    (2) Food? _____
    (3) Housing? _____
    (4) Others? (Please describe)_____

    _____

22. How often do your family members participate in housework?
    (1) All the time   (4) Seldom
    (2) Very often   (5) Never
    (3) Sometimes

23. How many hours do you spend a day in housework?
    (1) 10 or more hours   (4) 3-4 hours
    (2) 7-9 hours   (5) Less than 2 hours
    (3) 5-6 hours

24. Do you think your work in the apparel industry has contributed to your family financially?
    (1) Definitely yes   (4) Probably not
    (2) Probably yes   (5) Definitely not
    (3) Don't know

25. If your household did not need your financial contribution, would you give up this job immediately?
    (1) Definitely yes   (4) Probably not
    (2) Probably yes   (5) Definitely not
    (3) Don't know

26. If you have minor children, who takes care of them?

27. If you have children, how do you feel regarding time spent with your children?
    (1) Very satisfied   (4) Somewhat dissatisfied
    (2) Somewhat satisfied (5) Very dissatisfied
    (3) Don't know

28. How many hours do you spend taking care of your children a day (Including helping with homework, any activities for children, playing, etc.)?

29. Other than the time you spend caring for your children, how many hours do you spend in family-oriented activities per week?
    (1) How many hours do you spend in leisure activities with family?

    (2) How many hours do you spend in kinship obligations (Please describe your kinship obligation)?

    (3) Others (Please describe)

30. How satisfied are you with your family life?
    (1) Very satisfied   (4) Somewhat dissatisfied
    (2) Somewhat satisfied   (5) Very dissatisfied
    (3) Don't know

31. How much satisfaction do you get from your role within the family?
    (1) Very satisfied   (4) Somewhat dissatisfied
    (2) Somewhat satisfied   (5) Very dissatisfied
    (3) Don't know

32. Do you think women should be subordinate to their husbands in the family?
    (1) Definitely yes   (4) Probably not
    (2) Probably yes   (5) Definitely not
    (3) Don't know

33. How important are you to your family?
    (1) Very important   (4) Somewhat unimportant
    (2) Somewhat important   (5) Very unimportant
    (3) Don't know

Work Roles

34. How did you learn about this job?

35. What is the most important factor when you choose a company?
    (1) Salary   (4) Employer
    (2) Job position   (5) Working conditions
    (3) Location   (6) Others (Please describe)

36. How many hours do you work per week?

37. When do you work?
    (1) Early morning   (4) Evening
    (2) Morning   (5) Late night
    (3) Afternoon

38. Where do you mostly work?
    (1) Home   (3) Company
    (2) Home and company

39. What benefits does your company provide?

40. Does your company have a sick leave benefit?

41. Do you have medical insurance?
    (1) Yes   (2) No

42. Do you currently hold the same position in which you started?
    (1) Yes   (2) No

    If your answer is no, what kind of work do you do now?

43. How did you obtain the position?

44. How do you generally feel about the present working conditions?
    (1) Very satisfied   (4) Somewhat dissatisfied
    (2) Somewhat satisfied (5) Very dissatisfied
    (3) Don't know

45. Are you pleased with your position in the present company?
    (1) Definitely yes   (4) Probably not
    (2) Probably yes   (5) Definitely not
    (3) Don't know

46. How much satisfaction do you get from the company you work for?
    (1) A great deal   (4) A little
    (2) Moderate   (5) Not at all
    (3) Don't know

47. How long do you want to stay in the apparel industry?

48. Do you feel a sense of accomplishment from your job?
    (1) Definitely yes   (4) Probably not
    (2) Probably yes   (5) Definitely not
    (3) Don't know

49. Would you want your children to work in the apparel industry when they grow up?
    (1) Definitely yes   (4) Probably not
    (2) Probably yes   (5) Definitely not
    (3) Don't know

50. Do you think males get more advantages than females in the present company?
    (1) Yes   (2) No

    If your answer is yes, what kind of advantages do males have in the present company?

51. Do you think women should have less important positions than men at the work place?
    (1) Definitely yes
    (2) Probably yes
    (3) Don't know
    (4) Probably not
    (5) Definitely not

52. Do you think males get better positions than females in the present company?
    (1) Definitely yes
    (2) Probably yes
    (3) Don't know
    (4) Probably not
    (5) Definitely not

53. How many times have you changed companies in the apparel industry?

54. Do you think your present income is proportionate to the educational level you have achieved?
    (1) Definitely yes
    (2) Probably yes
    (3) Don't know
    (4) Probably not
    (5) Definitely not

55. Within the company, how do you feel about people's attitudes toward working women?
    (1) Very positively
    (2) Somewhat positively
    (3) Don't know
    (4) Somewhat negatively
    (5) Very negatively

56. How important is your position in your company?
    (1) Very important
    (2) Moderately important
    (3) Don't know
    (4) A little important
    (5) Not at all

57. Do you think you have a good relationship with your employer?
    (1) Definitely yes
    (2) Probably yes
    (3) Don't know
    (4) Probably not
    (5) Definitely not

58. What are the advantages and/or disadvantages of working in the apparel industry?

59. Do you have any problems working in this apparel company?

Social Roles

60. Do you think you have better living conditions in the United States than in Korea?
    - (1) Definitely better
    - (2) Probably better
    - (3) Don't know
    - (4) Probably worse
    - (5) Definitely worse

61. Do you think women should receive wages equal to those given men in the same job capacity?
    - (1) Definitely yes
    - (2) Probably yes
    - (3) Don't know
    - (4) Probably not
    - (5) Definitely not

62. In general, how do you feel about yourself in society?
    - (1) Very important
    - (2) Somewhat important
    - (3) Don't know
    - (4) Somewhat unimportant
    - (5) Very unimportant

63. Do you think you have contributed to the Korean-American community?
    - (1) Definitely yes
    - (2) Probably yes
    - (3) Don't know
    - (4) Probably not
    - (5) Definitely not

64. Do you think a woman's natural role is in domestic labor?
    - (1) Definitely yes
    - (2) Probably yes
    - (3) Don't know
    - (4) Probably not
    - (5) Definitely not

65. Do you think a man should be the breadwinner and a woman the housekeeper and child-raiser?
    (1) Definitely yes
    (2) Probably yes
    (3) Don't know
    (4) Probably not
    (5) Definitely not

66. How do you feel about women working in general?
    (1) Very positively
    (2) Somewhat positively
    (3) Don't know
    (4) Somewhat negatively
    (5) Very negatively

67. How do you feel about women's present status in the family as well as in our society?
    (1) Very satisfied
    (2) Somewhat satisfied
    (3) Don't know
    (4) Somewhat dissatisfied
    (5) Very dissatisfied

68. How would you describe the class to which you belong?
    (1) Upper class
    (2) Middle class
    (3) Lower class
    (4) Don't know

69. What did you hope to achieve by coming to the United States?

70. How successful have you been in terms of achieving your own aims in the United States?
    (1) Very successful
    (2) Moderately successful
    (3) Don't know
    (4) Little successful
    (5) Not at all successful

71. What has been the happiest time in your American life? (Please state freely.)

Perceived Health and Well Being

72. Do you have any illnesses at the present time?
    (1) Yes   (2) No

    If your answer is yes, please describe.

73. How many days have you felt sick during the last year?

74. How many days have you missed work during the last year?

75. How would you rate your health at the present time?
    (1) Excellent   (4) Poor
    (2) Good   (5) Very Poor
    (3) Fair

76. Do you worry a great deal about future illness?
    (1) Yes   (2) No

77. Psychologically, do you believe you are a strong woman?
    (1) Definitely yes   (4) Probably not
    (2) Probably yes   (5) Definitely not
    (3) Don't know

78. Physically, do you believe you are a strong woman?
    (1) Definitely yes   (4) Probably not
    (2) Probably yes   (5) Definitely not
    (3) Don't know

79. Do you believe you have a bright future?
    (1) Definitely yes   (4) Probably not
    (2) Probably yes   (5) Definitely not
    (3) Don't know

Thanks for your time.

REFERENCES

Almquist, Elizabeth M. *Minorities, Gender, and Work.* Lexingtion, Mass: D.C. Health and Company, 1979.

Alonso, Jose A. "The Domestic Clothing Workers in the Mexican Metropolis and Their Relation to Dependent Capitalism." Pp. 161-172 in *Women, Men and the International Division of Labor*, edited by June Nash and Maria Patricia Fernandez-Kelly. Albany, NY: State University of New York Press, 1983.

Aneshensel, C., R.R. Frerichs, and V.A. Clark. "Family Roles and Sex Differences in Depression." *Journal of Health and Social Behavior* 22:379-393, 1982.

Babbie, Earl. *The Practice of Social Research.* Belmont, CA: Wadsworth Publishing Company, 1989.

Bahr, Howard M., Bruch A. Chadwick, and Joseph H. Stauss. *American Ethnicity.* Lexington, Mass: D.C. Health and Company, 1979.

Bernard, Jessie. *The Female World from Global Perspective* Bloomington, IN: Indiana University Press, 1987.

Bleicher, Josef. *Contemporary Hermeneutics.* London, Boston and Henley: Routledge and Kegan Paul, 1980.

Bonacich, Edna, Mokerrom Hossain, and Jae-Hong Park. "Korean Immigrant Working Women in the Early 1980s." Pp. 219- 247 in *Korean Women in Transition: At Home and Abroad*, edited by Yu Eui-Young and Earl H. Phillips. Los Angeles, CA: Center for Korean-American and Korean Studies California State University, 1987.

Blau, Francine D. and Marianne A. Ferber. "Women in the Labor Market." Pp. 19-49 in *Women and Work: An Annual Review*, Vol. 1, edited by Laurie Larwood, Ann H. Stromberg and Barbara A. Gutek. Beverly Hills, CA: Sage Publications, Inc., 1985.

Bureau of Public Affairs. *Background Notes.* Edited by Peter A. Knecht. Washington, DC: United States Department of State, Office of Public Communications, 1987.

Cabezas, Amado and Gary Kawaguchi. "Empirical Evidence for Continuing Asian American Income Inequality: The Human Capital Model and Labor Market Segmentation." Pp. 145-164 in *Reflections on Shattered Windows: Promises and Prospects for Asian American Studies*, edited by Gary Y. Okihiro, Shirley Hune, Arthur A. Hansen, and John M. Liu. Seattle, WA: Washington State University Press, 1988.

Chai, Alice Yun. "Women's History in Public: 'Picture Brides' of Hawaii." *Women's Studies Quarterly* 1 & 2:51-63, 1988.

Choy, Bong-Youn. *Koreans in America*. Chicago, Ill: Nelson-Hall, 1979.

Collins, Randall. *Theoretical Sociology*. Orlando, FL: Harcourt Brace Jovanovich Publishers, 1988.

Coser, Lewis A. *Masters of Sociological Thought*. New York: Harcourt Brace Jovanovich Publishers, 1977.

Coyle, Angela. "Sex and Skill in the Organization of the Clothing Industry." Pp. 10-26 in *Work, Women and the Labour Market*, edited by Jackie West. London: Routledge & Kegan Paul, 1982.

Cox, Oliver Cromwell. *Capitalism As a System*. New York: Monthly Review Press, 1964.

Dalla Costa, Mariaosa. "Women and the Subversion of Community." *Radical America* Vol. 6, No. 1:67-103, 1972.

Daniels, Roger. *Asian America: Chinese and Japanese in the United States since 1850*. Seattle, WA: University of Washington Press, 1988.

de Beauvoir, Simone De. *The Second Sex*. New York: Alfred A. Knopf. B, 1957.

Denzin, Norman K. *The Research Act: A Theoretical Introduction to Sociological Methods*. New York: McGraw-Hill Book Company, 1978.

Donovan, Josephine. *Feminist Theory: The Intellectual Traditions of American Feminism*. New York: Frederick Ungar Publishing Co., 1985.

Eisenstein, Hester. *Contemporary Feminist Thought*. Boston, Mass: G. K. Hall & Co., 1983.

Engels, Frederick. *The Origin of the Family, Private Property and the State*. New York: International Publishers, 1972.

Enloe, Cynthia H. "Women Textile Workers in the Militarization of Southeast Asia." Pp. 407-425 in *Women, Men, and the International Division of Labor*, edited by June Nash and Maria Patricia Fernandez-Kelly. Albany, NY: State University of New York Press, 1983.

Feagin, Joe R. and Clairece Booher Feagin. *Racial and Ethnic Relations*. Englewood Cliffs, NJ: Prentice Hall, 1993.

Fox, Mary Frank and Sharlene Hesse-Biber (Eds.). *Women at Work*. Mayfield Publishing Company, 1984.

Glaser Barney G. and Anselm L. Strauss. *The Discovery of Grounded Theory: Strategies for Qualitative Research*. New York: Aldine De Gruyter, 1967.

Gorden, Raymond. *Interviewing: Strategy, Techniques, and Tactics*. Chicago, Ill: The Dorsey Press, 1987.

Gore, Susan and Thomas W. Mangione. "Social Roles, Sex Roles and Psychological Distress." *Journal of Health and Social Behavior* 24:300-312, 1983.

Hartmann, Heidi. "The Unhappy Marriage of Marxism and Feminism: Towards a More Progressive Union." Pp. 1-41 in *Women and Revolution*, edited by Lydia Sargent. Boston, MA: South End Press, 1981.

Haynes, Suzanne G. and Manning Feinleib. "Women, Work and Coronary Heart Disease: Prospective Findings from the Framingham Heart Study." *American Journal of Public Health* Vol. 70, No. 2:133-141, 1980.

Hoel, Barbro. "Contemporary Clothing 'Sweatshops', Asian Female Labour and Collective Organization." Pp. 80-98 in *Work, Women and the Labour Market*, edited by Jackie West. London: Routledge & Kegan Paul, 1982.

Hughey, A.M. "The Incomes of Recent Female Immigrants to the United States." *Social Science Quarterly* Vol. 17, No. 2:383-390, 1990.

Hunter, Herbert M. and Sameer Y. Abraham (Eds.). *Race, Class, and the World System: The Sociology of Oliver C. Cox*. New York: Monthly Review Press, 1987.

Hurh, Won Moo and Kwang Chung Kim. "Race Relations Paradigms and Korean American Research: A Sociology of Knowledge Perspective." Pp. 219-245 in *Koreans in Los Angeles Prospects and Promises*, edited by Eui-Young Yu et al. Los Angeles, CA:

Koryo Research Institute, 1982.
Hurh, Won M. and Kwang Chung Kim. *Koreans Immigrants in America*. Cranbury, NJ: Associated University Presses, 1984.
Kahn- Hut, Rachel., Arlene Kaplan Daniels., and Richard Colvard (Eds.). *Women and Work: Problems and Perspectives*. New York: Oxford University Press, 1982.
Kandel, D.B., M.Davies, and V.H.Raveis. "The Stressfulness of Daily Social Roles for Women." *Journal of Health and Social Behavior* 26:64-78, 1985.
Kaufman, Bruce E. *The Economics of Labor Markets*. Orlando, FL: The Dryden Press, 1991.
Kim, Bernice Bong Hee. "The Korean in Hawaii." Pp. 109-113 in *The Korean in America 1882-1974*, edited by Kim, Hyung-Chan and Patterson, Wayne. New York: Oceana Publications, Inc., 1984.
Kim, Hyung-Chan. "Some Aspect of Social Demography of Korean Americans." Pp. 109-126 in *The Korean Diaspora: Historical and Sociological Studies of Korean Immigration and Assimilation in North America*, edited by Hyung-Chang Kim. Santa Barbara, CA: ABC-Clio, Inc., 1977.
_____. "Koreans in the United States." Pp. 13-22 in *Dictionary of Asian American History*, edited by Hyung-Chan Kim. New York: Greenwood Press, 1986.
Kim, Hyung-Chan and Wayne Patterson. *The Koreans in America 1882-1974: A Chronology and Fact Book*. New York: Dobbs Ferry, 1974.
Kim, Kwang Chung and Won Moo Hurh. "Employment of Korean Immigrant Wives and the Division of Household Tasks." Pp. 199-218 in *Korean Women in Transition*, edited by Eui-Young Yu and Eark H. Phillips. Los Angeles, CA: Center for Korean-American and Korean Studies, California State University, 1987.
Kim, Yung-Chung (Ed.). *Women of Korea: A History from Ancient Times to 1945*. Seoul, Korea: Ewha Womans University Press, 1976.
Klemm, David E. *The Hermeneutical Theory of Paul Ricoeur*. Lewisburg: Bucknell University Press, 1983.
Koh, Yang Kon. *An Exploratory Study of Filial Support and the Use of Formal Services among the Korean Aged in New York City*. Unpublished Doctoral Dissertation. Florida State University,

Tallahassee, 1983.
Koh, Hesung Chun. "Korean Women, Conflict, and Change: An Approach to Development Planning." Pp. 159-174 in *Korean Women: View from the Inner Room*, edited by Laurel Kendall and Mark Peterson. New Haven, CT: East Rock Press, Inc., 1983.
Kotler, Pamela and Deborah Lee Wingard. "The Effect of Occupational, Marital and Parental Roles on Mortality: The Alameda County Study." *American Journal of Public Health* 79:607-612, 1989.
Labaw, Patricia. *Advanced Questionnaire Design.* Cambridege, MA: Abt Books, 1985.
Lerner, Gerda. *The Creation of Patriarchy.* New York: Oxford University Press, 1986.
Levi-Strauss, Claude. *The Elementary Structures of Kinship.* Boston, MA: Beacon Press, 1969.
Light, Ivan and Edna Bonacich. *Immigrant Entrepreneurs: Koreans in Los Angeles 1965-1982.* Berkeley and Los Angeles, CA: University of California Press, 1988.
Lim, Linda Y.C. "The Dilemma of Third-World Women Workers in Multinational Factories." Pp. 70-91 in *Women, Men, and the International Division of Labor*, edited by June Nash and Maria Particia Fernandez-Kelly. Albany, NY: State University of New York Press, 1983.
Linge, David E. (Ed.). *Philosophical Hermeneutics: Hans-Georg Gadamer.* Los Angeles, CA: University of California Press, Ltd., 1977.
Mangiafico, Luciano. *Contemporary American Immigrants: Patterns of Filipino, Korean, and Chinese Settlement in the United States.* New York: Praeger, 1988.
Marx, Karl. *Capital: A Critical Analysis of Capitalist Production.* Frederick Engels (Ed.), New York: International Publishers, 1939.
McAllister, Ian. "Gender and the Household Division of Labor: Employment and Earnings Variations in Australia." *Work and Occupations* Vol. 17, No. 1:79-99, 1990.
Mead, George H. *Mind, Self, and Society: From the Standpoint of a Social Behaviorist.* Charles W. Morris (Ed.) Chicago, ILL: The University of Chicago Press, 1934.
Melendy, Howard B. *Asians in America: Filipinos, Koreans, and East Indians.* Boston, Mass: Twayne Publishers, 1977.

Millett, Kate. *Sexual Politics*. New York: Ballantine Books, 1970.
Min, Pyong Gap. "The Korean American Family." Pp. 199-229 in *Ethnic Families in America: Patterns and Variations*, edited by Charles H. Mindel, Robert W. Habenstein, and Roosevelt Wright, Jr. New York: Elsevier Science Publishing Co., Inc., 1988.
Mise, Maria. *Patriarchy and Accumulation on a World Scale: Women in the International Division of Labour*. London United Kingdom: Zed Books Ltd., 1986.
Mitchell, Juliet. *Psychoanalysis and Feminism*. New York: Pantheon Books, 1974.
Mitter, Swasti. *Common Fate Common Bond: Women in the Global Economy*. Wolfeboro, NH: Pluto Press, 1986.
Nathanson, Constance A. "Social Roles and Health Status among Women: The Significance of Employment." *Social Science and Medicine* Vol. 14A:463-471, 1980.
Nieva, Veronica F. "Work and Family Linkages." Pp. 162-190 in *Women and Work: An Annual Review* (Vol. 1), edited by Laurie Larwood, Ann H. Strombery, and Barbara A. Gutek. Beverly Hills, CA: Sage Publications, 1985.
Nieva, Veronica F. and Gutek, Barbara A. *Women and Work: A Psychological Perspective*. New York: Praeger Publishers, Inc., 1981.
Phelps, Linda. "Patriarchy and Capitalism." Pp. 161-173 in *Building Feminist Theory: Essays from Quest*, introduce by Charlotte Bunch. New York: Longman, 1981.
Pleck, Joseph H. "The Work-Family Role System." Pp. 101-110 in *Women and Work*, edited by Kahn-Hut Rachel. New York: Oxford University Press, 1982.
Polkinghorne, Donald. *Methodology for the Human Sciences: Systems of Inquiry*. Albany, NY: State University of New York Press, 1983.
Rapoport, Rhona and Robert N. Rapoport. "The Dual Career Family: A Variant Pattern and Social Change." *Human Relations* Vol. 22: 3-30, 1969.
Reich, Michael., David M. Gordon., and Richard C. Edwards. "A Theory of Labor Market Segmentation." Pp. 232-241 in *The Economics of Women and Work*, edited by Amsden Alice. New York: St. Martin's Press, 1980.

Ricoeur, Paul. *The Symbolism of Evil.* Translated Emerson Buchanan. Boston, Mass: Beacon Press, 1967.

_____. "Existence and Hermeneutic." Pp. 101-119 in *The Philosophy of Paul Ricoeur*, edited by Reagan Charles E. and Steward David. Boston, Mass: Boston Press, 1978a.

_____. "Metaphor and the Main Problem of Hermeneutics." Pp. 134-148 in *The Philosophy of Paul Ricoeur*, edited by Reagan Charles E. and Steward David. Boston, Mass: Boston Press, 1978b.

_____. "Explanation and Understanding: On Some Remarkable Connections Among the Theory of the Text, Theory of Action, and Theory of History." Pp. 149-166 in *The Philosophy of Paul Ricoeur*, edited by Reagan Charles E. and Steward David. Boston, Mass: Boston Press, 1978c.

_____. "Hermeneutics and the Critique of Ideology." Pp. 300-339 in *Hermeneutics and Modern Philosophy*, edited by Brice R. Wachterhauser. Albany, NY: State University of New York Press, 1986.

Ritzer, George. *Sociological Theory.* New York: Alfred A. Knopf, Inc., 1988.

Ross, Catherine E. and John Mirowsky. "Child Care and Emotional Adjustment of Wives' Employment." *Journal of Health and Social Behavior* Vol. 29:127-138, 1988.

Rothman, Robert A. *Working Sociological Perspectives.* Englewood Cliffs, NJ: Prentice-Hall, Inc., 1987.

Scazoni, John. *Opportunity and the Family.* New York: Free Press, 1970.

Schutz, Alfred. *Collected Papers.* Vol.II. edited and introduced by Arvid Brodersen. The Hague, Netherlands: Martinus Nijhoff, 1976.

Shin, Eui Hang. "Interracially Married Korean Women in the United States: An Analysis Based on Hypergame-Exchange Theory." Pp. 249-274 in *Korean Women in Transition: At Home and Abroad*, edited by Eui-Young Yu and Earl H. Phillips. Los Angeles, CA: Center for Korean-American and Korean Studies, California State University, 1987.

Smith, Dorothy E. *The Everyday World As Problematic: A Feminist Sociology.* Boston, Mass: Northeastern University Press, 1987.

Smith, Ralph E. "The Movement of Women into the Labor Force." Pp. 1-29 in *The Subtle Revolution: Women at Work*, edited by Ralph E. Smith. Washington, DC: The Urban Institute, 1979.

Sorensen, Clark. "Women, Men; Inside, Outside: The Division of Labor in Rural Central Korea." Pp. 63-78 in *Korean Women: View from the Inner Room*, edited by Laurel Kendall and Mark Peterson. New Haven, CT: East Rock Press, Inc., 1983.

Statistical Abstract of the United States. 109th edition, Washington, DC: U.S. Department of Commerce Bureau of Census, 1989.

Sung, Betty Lee. *A Survey of Chinese-American Manpower and Employment*. New York: Praeger Publishers, Inc., 1976.

Takaki, Ronald. *Strangers From a Different Shore: History of Asian Americans*. Boston, MA: Little, Brown and Company, 1989.

Tompson, John B. (Ed.). *Paul Ricoeur Hermeneutics and the Human Sciences: Essays on Language, Action and Interpretation*. New York: Cambridge University Press, 1981.

Tong, Rosemarie. *Feminist Thought: A Comprehensive Introduction*. Boulder, CO: Westview Press, 1989.

Turner, Jonathan H., Leonard Beeghley, and Charles H. Powers. *The Emergence of Sociological Theory*. Chicago, Ill: The Dorsey Press, 1989.

Um, Shin Ja. "Historical Korean 'Picture Brides' for Korean-Hawaiian Workers: A Hermeneutic Approach." Paper presented at the Annual Meeting of the Society for Phenomenology and Human Sciences, Duquesne University in Pittsburgh, Pennsylvania: October 12-15, 1989.

U.S. Bureau of the Census. *Supplementary Report Asian and Pacific Islander Population by State: 1980*. Census of Population, PC 80-S1-12. Washington, DC: U.S. Government Printing Office, 1983.

_____. *General Population Characteristics, Texas*, Census of Population, CP-1-45. Washington, DC: U.S. Goverment Printing Office, 1992.

U.S. Department of Commerce. *Statistical Abstract of the United States: The National Data Book*. Washington, DC: U.S. Bureau of the Census, 1990.

_____. *U.S. Industrial Outlook: Prospects for 350 industries with 450 tables and charts*. WA: U.S. Bureau of the Census, 1991.

_____. *We the American Asians*. WE-3 (September), Washington, DC: U.S. Bureau of the Census, 1993.

Vanek, Joann. "Time Spent in Housework." Pp. 82-90 in *The Economics of Women and Work*, edited by Smsden, Alice H. New York: St. Martin's Press, 1980.

Vazquez, Mario F. "Immigrant Workers and the Apparel Manufacturing Industry in Southern California." Pp. 85-96 in *Mexican Immigrant Workers in the U.S.*, edited by Antonio Rios-Bustamante. Los Angeles, CA: Chicano Studies Research Center Publications, 1981.

Verbrugge, Lois, M. "Multiple Roles and Physical Health of Women and Men." *Journal of Health and Social Behavior* Vol. 24 (March):16-30, 1983.

Voydanoff, Patricia. *Work and Family Life*. Family Studies Text Series 6. Newbury Park, CA: Sage Publications, Inc, 1987.

Wagner, Helmut R. *Phenomenology of Consciousness and Sociology of the Life-world: An Introductory Study*. Alberta: The University of Alberta Press, 1983.

Weedon, Chris. *Feminist Practice and Poststructuralist Theory*. New York: Basil Blackwell, 1987.

Wiseman, Jacqueline P. and Aron Marcis S. *Field Projects for Sociology Students*. San Francisco, CA: Canfield Press, 1970.

Yang, Eun Sik. 1987. "Korean Women in America: 1903 - 1930." Pp. 167-181 in *Korean Women in Transition at Home and Abroad*, edited by Eui-Young Yu and Eark H. Phillips. Los Angeles, CA: Center for Korean-American and Korean Studies, California State University, 1987.

Yoon, Soon Young S. "The Role of Korean Women in National Development." Pp. 157-167 in *Virtues in Conflict: Tradition and the Korean Woman Today*, edited by Sandra Mattielli. Seoul, Korea: Samhwa Publishing Co., Ltd., 1977.

Yun, Yo-jun. 1977. "Early History of Korean Immigration to America." Pp. 33-46 in *The Korean Diaspora: Historical and Sociological Studies of Korean Immigration and Assimilation in North America*, edited by Hyung-Chang Kim. Santa Barbara, CA: ABC-Clio, Inc.

Zavella, Patricia. *Women's Work & Chicano Families: Cannery Workers of the Santa Clara Valley*. Ithaca, NY: Cornell University Press, 1987.

INDEX

Acculturation, 31
Adaptation, 20
Ahn chuin, 106
Alienation, 8, 9, 64, 117
Apparel company, 13, 15, 37-38, 42-43, 51, 64, 75, 77-79, 104, 113, 115
Apparel industry, 1-2, 13-15, 17, 28, 31-34, 36, 39-44, 51-53, 55, 57, 63-65, 72,-80, 92, 96, 99-101, 103-106, 110-115, 120
   advantages and disadvantages of working, 64, 75-76, 103-104, 115
   benefits, 79, 104
   figurative meanings, 105
   job turnover, 71-72, 79
   recruitment, 42
   wages, 43
   working conditions, 38-39, 70, 72, 74, 76, 78, 104, 115
   working hours, 42, 63, 76, 115
   working places, 43
Appropriation, 39, 99, 106
Asian immigrants, 2, 119
Assimilation, 20
Bourgeois, 25
Cannery workers, 30
Capital, 5, 7-9, 15, 29, 72, 105
Capitalism, 5, 7-9, 15, 29, 108, 17, 119
Capitalist, 7-8,
Capitalist system, 8, 108
Child care, 12, 14, 22, 54-55, 59-61, 63-64, 101, 113-114, 120
Ch'ima param, 107

Class oppression, 7
Class struggle, 7
Cloth, 120
Clothing industry, 28-29
Competition, 77, 104, 106
Confucian philosophy, 21
Discrimination, 4, 18-19, 25, 27, 82
Division of household, 24
Division of labor, 3, 6-8, 15, 26-27, 32
Domestic labor, 80, 82-83, 107
Depression, 11-12, 77
Dual career family, 23
English proficiency, 31, 49
English language, 14, 31, 41, 49, 53, 59-61, 64, 74, 76, 100-101, 105, 113, 120
Exploitation, 7-8, 21, 30, 77, 108
Extended family, 44, 53
Family cohesion, 10
Familial roles, 1, 13-15, 24, 32, 41, 54-44, 58, 98, 103, 108, 111, 113-114, 117, 119
Family roles, 10-12, 15, 22-23, 108, 113, 116
Feminism, 1, 9, 109
Feminist, 3, 7, 25, 119, 120
Feminist perspective, 54, 119
Feministic inclinations, 120
Garment companies, 36, 42, 65, 76, 104, 112
Garment industry, 28-30, 32, 43, 48, 65, 67, 74, 76, 103-104, 106, 113, 117, 119-120
Garment job, 100, 103

Garment workers, 5, 117
Gender, 5, 7-9, 11-12, 15, 22-23, 25-27, 30-32, 64, 73, 82-83, 86, 117, 119
Gender role, 31, 54, 84, 107, 110, 117, 119-120,
  conception of, 107
  expectations, 54
Health, 1, 5, 10-11, 15-16, 79, 92-93, 95, 97, 104, 116, 120
  mental, 10-11
  perceived, 1, 13-16, 33-34, 41, 92, 111, 116
  physical, 10-11, 15, 92, 95, 97-98, 104, 116
  psychological, 12, 15, 92, 95, 97, 104, 116
Hermeneutic, 34-36, 38-39, 98-99, 108, 110, 112
Hierarchical structure, 119
Hierarchical relations, 25
Immigration Act, 19-20
Immigration law, 20, 29
Immigration and Naturalization Act, 1
Inequality, 25
Key, 119
Kinship, 62, 114
Korean, 105, 107
  educational attainment, 48, 110
  family, 55, 109-110
  language, 61, 106
  society, 55, 82, 117, 120
  traditional family, 55, 83, 102
Korean emigration, 19
Korean immigrants, 2, 4, 17-21, 32
  family, 75, 100-101
  living conditions, 105
Korean immigration, 17-18, 20, 31, 50
  patterns of, 17, 31, 111
Korean immigrant women, 1-2, 13-15, 17, 20-22, 24, 31-32, 37, 42, 55, 99 111, 117, 120
Korean National Association, 19
Korean Texas Garment Contractor's Association, 36, 42, 77, 112
Korean War, 19
Korean women, 1, 2, 20-22, 54, 100, 105, 106-108, 116, 117, 119
  activities, 105, 106
  attitude, 105
  married women, 41, 54, 75, 105, 110-111, 116-117
  occupational conditions in Korea, 100
  perspectives, 105
  psychological strength, 108
  roles, 55, 117
  social status, 107, 117
  social support networks in the U.S. 100-101
Koryo dynasty, 107
Labor force, 1, 22-25, 27-28, 30, 42, 80, 101
Labor-force participation, 10, 24, 30-31, 54, 64
  women's, 109
Labor market, 3-5, 17, 23-24, 27-28, 31
Labor-market approach, 5-6
Labor market segmentation, 3, 15, 43, 117
Language handicap, 101
Leisure activities, 62, 95-96, 114
Materialism, 9
Matrifocal, 44, 53
Marxism, 9
Marxian feminist, 3, 7-9, 15
Marxian feminist theory, 3, 7, 15
Marxist theory, 9
Mobility, 5

Multi-method approach, 33, 35, 103, 111
Nuclear family, 44, 53-54, 112
Oppression, 7, 15, 22, 25-26, 31, 108
Pakkat chuin, 106
Patriarchal family, 24-25, 54-55, 83
Patriarchal society, 1, 55, 107, 109
Patriarchal structure, 31, 43, 55, 105-106, 108-110, 117-120
Patriarchal systems, 27, 86, 108
Patriarchal relations, 27
Patriarchy, 7, 17, 24-27, 31-32, 108, 110-117
definition of, 25
Picture brides, 18, 21-22, 119-120
Proletarian, 7
Proletariat, 25
Role, 1, 9-12, 22-24, 26, 32, 34, 55, 80, 83, 99, 102-103, 105-109, 116, 120
conflict, 23
man's 80, 84-85, 107, 115, 117
multiple roles, 10-11, 15, 33, 97, 117
primary, 25, 109
secondary, 25, 109
traditional women's, 102, 105, 109
woman's, 1, 10, 15, 17, 20, 22, 25, 31-32, 80, 84-85, 115, 117-118
See also familial roles; social roles; work roles
Role theory, 3, 9, 15
Salary, 57, 65-66, 79, 114
Self, 3, 9-10, 15, 55, 88-89
Segmentation, 3-5
primary, 3-5
race, 3-4
secondary, 3-5
sex, 3, 5
Segmentation theory, 5
Self-esteem, 110
Seven grounds, 116
Sewer, 29, 51, 53, 65, 67, 76, 78-79, 102, 113,
home, 36, 38, 76, 78-79, 102, 115
Sewing, 36-38, 41-43, 50, 55, 57, 60, 64-65, 76-79, 82, 96, 101
Sex role, 26, 55, 110, 120
conception, 109-110, 120
expectations, 110
segregation, 120
Shiage, 43, 67
Social class, 18, 23, 80-81, 103, 107
Social mobility, 103, 109
Social roles, 1, 12-15, 41, 80, 98, 111, 115
Socialization, 54, 110, 117
Society, 1, 3, 9-10, 14-15, 19, 25, 88-89, 103, 107-108, 115-116, 120
Asian, 1
Korean, 117
Support networks, 100-101
Text, 34-35. 38-39, 100, 102-103, 106, 108-109
Textile workers, 28
Thread, 120
Triangulation 33, 35
War bride, 20
Woman's natural role, 25, 80, 82-84, 107, 115
Work roles, 1-2, 12-13, 32, 41, 54, 63, 98, 105-106, 108, 110-111, 114
World-system, 8
Yi Dynasty, 107, 116

About the Author

Shin Ja Um is currently a lecturer at Soong Sil University in Seoul, Korea, where she received a B.A. in English literature and an M.A. in social work. Born and raised in Seoul, she went to the United States and completed her graduate work in sociology at Texas Woman's University in Denton, Texas. She received an M.A. and a Ph.D. in sociology from Texas Woman's University.